Alive at 35

Redefining Self-Worth and Discovering What Love Is.

By: Malissa Penick

CONTENTS

Introduction

The person I am today was shaped by my personal experiences and education. Given my background, most would feel like I hit the poverty power ball. After my journey, I see the beauty in the disaster. I want to thank every single person from the ones who were a lesson to the ones who are a blessing. Every single situation shaped me into the person I am now. I can now see it as my beautiful disaster. It is easy to give up in the disaster, it takes strength to get to where you see the beauty in it. Most would want to give up, like I wanted to quite often. I used to feel ashamed to discuss anything personal coming from such a toxic environment until I developed self-awareness and realized it isn't about me. My life went from me looking at it like a disaster to me working on myself and can now see only the beauty in my disaster. It is my beautiful disaster.

Although I am grateful for the person I am and continue to become, it took a while to get here. I don't know about you, but my expectations on being an adult were not properly prepared for me to experience on a healthy level from childhood. No judgment to my mother nor father and I would like to believe they did the best they could with what they had. I remember how they would often ask themselves out loud why certain things were happening to them. I learned instead to look at it from a perspective of, what is this situation trying to teach me? The right perspective and the right questions can change everything. After redefining everything in my life, I feel as if I am experiencing it for the first time. Hopefully, we can experience this journey together so we can all fall in love with becoming the best version of ourselves. Let's dive in!

Poem: I see you; I hear you.

To: Adult Self
From: Inner Child

This house isn't a home; I feel constantly alone.
Parents physically here, but remain mentally gone.

My existence is invisible to their eyes.
I wonder if I am loud enough will they hear my cries.

Where is my protection?

Help me. I am drowning in pain.
I'd rather end it all, then question if I am the one insane.
Remaining too self-involved to question what's on my brain.

Confusions show.
As their hate for each other continues to grow.

I have a voice, but they seem to not care.
Screaming on the inside, they seem so unaware.

The energy all around is dark. This is too much for a child to bare.
As I lay on my back looking up with a watery stare.

Wondering where God is…
I need you. Why on earth am I here?
Blaming him with so much anger and hate.
Who else do I look to when I desperately want to escape?

I should kill myself. There's no one around for a debate.
I wouldn't be missed; pretty sure I was a mistake.

As I swallow all the pills.
Please forgive me. This is no way to live.

The air feels heavy. There is no longer a disguise.
My body is numb all over. That comes as no surprise.
Her eyes can't lie. She remains fixated on the sunrise.

One question remains...
Is she awake?
Or is she stuck in a dream state?

Inner Child - the kid still alive inside each grown-up desperate to be seen and heard. Conveys unhealed feelings. Unwittingly looks for adoration and approval.

Here I am sitting in class for my life skills program. This program was one of many things I was trying after hitting what appears to be rock bottom in my life. At this point, I didn't know what to believe anymore. I was lost in confusion with a distorted view of how I got to this point. So, I am sitting in my class trying to learn more about all the toxic people of my past. You know, so I can avoid anyone like them moving forward. I remember thinking this should resolve all the issues in my life. I often wondered why I was continuing to attract certain types of people within my life. At this point, I was open to the possibility of it being me. I was hard on myself in that way. After years of self-help books and programs and being open to new outcomes with positivity, I was at a loss for what was going on with me. I guess the pain was too overwhelming for reflection. This pain is the kind of pain that forces you to do whatever it takes to push out by any means. Being open for change allowed me to feel this and this class was a chance at reflection. I remember sitting there after a self-reflection assignment and in that moment realizing...I'm just as fucked up as they are. WOW! How did I miss this? How did this happen? I knew exactly where to start in my questioning. There is one common denominator throughout it all...me. My questions became overwhelming, which led me into a state of depression.

Eventually, I was ready to reflect on these questions again. It happened after ending a relationship I was in for nearly a decade. When you have no other choice after being in a dark place, you will leave anything that does not feed your soul. Turns out that was accurate for my situation. I never understood how people could walk away from situations unplanned with nothing. Until now...I walked away knowing I would be a single mom with only $200 to my name and no support in sight.

I was working the night shift at a well-known hospital in Northern California. Working 12-hour night shifts can be challenging, so I tried to make it least complicated as possible. To do that, I started a 6 on 8 off schedule. This consisted of me working six 12- hour night shifts in a row and then having 8 off if overtime wasn't picked up. The day I walked away from my relationship, I was in the middle of my 6-night stretch. I remember thinking how so much had changed about myself beyond recognition. I was thousands of miles away from my hometown, where most of my family was at. I had recently moved from SoCal to NorCal and I didn't know many people yet. I remember the life-changing moment I had from talking to my therapist. Once I told her about the harsh realities of my present relationship at the time and past childhood. It didn't take her long to see the situation from a clear view. Funny how that happens the further away from people and situations you are, I guess it takes away people being emotionally involved. This makes it easier to rationalize things. She did just that with this life-changing statement. She said,

"Malissa, it sounds like your ex is just like your father." Yes, she was referring to my biological father, the one with Narcissistic Traits who abused the entire household in my childhood.

Once I realized that I play a role in attracting toxic people, this forced me to want to learn everything I could about myself to become more self-aware. This also forced me to look into something I have avoided for years…my toxic childhood. I had no choice. Things from my childhood were spilling into my adulthood and felt like I was experiencing the same things on repeat.

Because I was stuck in my personal modern-day Groundhog Day.

The hardest thing to process about this entire situation was realizing I had no self-worth. I thought I did. When and how did this happen? I guess around the time I stopped taking responsibility for myself, the respect left shortly after. As long as I was projecting all of my issues onto everyone else, I didn't have to be held responsible for anything. Where did my victim mentally come from suddenly, I don't recall always being this way? Externally seeking solutions for things beyond my control. It wasn't until I took responsibility for my part in things and working on myself, I noticed a shift. Living in the solution from within felt great! After that, my emotions were a roller coaster. Which meant I still needed to work on the root of my issues. How did I keep finding myself in situations that made me feel a certain way based upon how others treated me? My self-worth was measured based upon how others treated me and this constantly put me into a state of feeling unworthiness and unloved.

Why was I searching for love in external validation? How did I learn this way of being? Childhood. Usually, we look at parents as being superheroes, as if they can do no wrong. Which results in us never questioning the things they do and say. Until you have to, the biggest lesson upon my discoveries was realizing that the people who I saw as parents didn't teach me, show me, or behave lovingly because they didn't know how to. Maybe they assumed they did. How can they love me when they never loved themselves? I could either risk repeating that same cycle or I can learn for myself and from their mistakes.

A lot of intimidating barriers prevent you from getting to know yourself all over again. The human race constantly evolves and there are always new things we have to learn in that evolution. What happens when you stop learning about yourself when you are always seeking external validation to feel whole or feeling as if you have no control over your own life?

This book removes the intimidating barriers from people feeling lonely instead of alone and offers the simple steps and psychology in redefining your self- worth by giving you a chance to fall in love with yourself to always feel whole and free whether single or not.

Make small, realistic, achievable changes in your life. Remember, it is a marathon, not a sprint...be gentle with yourself.

I've heard people say to be single for a while after a relationship. Well, how long is a while and is it situational based? I've also heard sayings to get under the next person as soon as possible to get over the last. These sayings have been passed on from generation to generation without many questionings anything about it. I guess we all have assumed to understand what that means in our own way. This book explains the grey area...the how. This book is for people who want clarification and details on how to be single, how to feel whole in being alone and what to do to become more self-aware so you can discover love from the core. You'll learn how responsibility breeds empowerment. Self-awareness will become consistent in your life. You will take your redefined self-worth into relationships and out of relationships with a better understanding of not just yourself, but others.

"The more you know yourself, the more patience you have for what you see in others."

— Erik Erikson

This book is not for people who want a quick fix in their lives. This is a lifelong commitment and from a choice you must make to get to know yourself so it has you falling in love with you for the first time or all over again.

"*You are the greatest project you will ever get to work on. Take your time. Create magic.*" – Morgan Harper Nichols

This book helps people realize that you can wake up at any age and redefine your self-worth. Only then will you feel alive.

Let's get started in the process of getting to know ourselves fully.

One of the hardest things I've ever had to do is grieve two parents who are still living. The harsh reality is they were incapable of loving us, their children, because they never loved their selves. I didn't know the importance of self-love until now. I finally feel alive.

What is a father's role? Fathers, like mothers, are pillars in developing a youngster's passionate prosperity. Youngsters look to their dads to set out the principles and uphold them. They likewise look to their dads to give a sentiment of security, both physical and mentally. A father's love contributes as much and sometimes more to a child's development as does a mother's love. Dependable on acceptance or rejection during their childhood. An involved father promotes inner growth and strength. At the point when fathers are warm and strong, it significantly influences a youngster's psychological and social turn of events. It additionally ingrains a general feeling of prosperity and self-assurance. Hmm, I guess my father never received his job description. How could something that is supposed to come so naturally end up a total miss?

People nowadays fail to realize the importance of mental health. Sometimes there is a voice talking to you, and instead of thinking you are crazy, it is a good idea to figure out what that voice is saying and why? Basically, what are you thinking and why are you thinking it? During my journey of self-awareness and rediscovering what love meant I struggled with something most struggle with. You hear these sayings to do what it takes to numb that feeling of pain, anger, victim mentality. What happened to the voice that questions why you feel that way? Ignoring the voice and numbing the pain isn't dealing with the primary issue. And not dealing with the primary issue is an indication you will feel these feelings again and constantly hear negative self-talk. The problem is if you hear that voice long enough matched to those feelings…you believe every negative thing it has been feeding you. I woke up one day realizing somewhere along the way I stopped loving myself. Maybe this was linked to my depression or complex PTSD from childhood. Was this learned? How do I truly feel about myself? Oddly enough, it was the day I discovered my parents were deemed incapable of ever loving me. I grew up with emotionally immature parents with some narcissistic traits…I didn't know this until my adult life. It took me stepping outside the situation, thousands of miles away to discover this. There just might be something to the saying that we see things clearer once stepping out of it to observe it from an objective standpoint. I remember my emotional flood day like it was yesterday. Emotional flood day is when you receive a whole bunch of information over time and on this day, you are able to process things for what they are and tie it back into so many situations within your life. Like you get your memory of things for the first time. So emotionally drowning and full of tears. I remember thinking I no longer want to be familiar with emotional pain, and I can do without questioning every decision I make out of anger. This time was different; this time the road led me to what I would consider my breaking point. I was forced to decide. I chose me, for the first time. Now, how do I go about doing this? Where do I get started? So many questions I had that were never addressed before. I had nothing to lose and everything to gain. I was determined to do whatever it takes to become who I am truly meant to be. I know this meant reliving my childhood traumas up to my adulthood decisions and finally being the one responsible for my own life. Meaning after this journey, I can do something I have been avoiding my entire life...self-awareness to break up with my toxic parents and discovering what self-love means to me.

Although physical abuse can be detrimental. Other forms of abuse can be worse. With physical, at least you can see the scars and they heal over time, while mental/emotional abuse unchecked can lead to body harm and the scars are invisible to everyone else but runs deep within.

I understand women who struggle with how to feel free and how to happily be single. These are questions I didn't have until my adult life. I grew up in a loveless household around women with the idea to always be in a relationship…avoid being single by any means. I didn't think that most people struggle with being alone. So much I didn't know growing up. I've been around women known for always being in a relationship. Later I learned, being alone would equate for them having to face who they truly are. I get it is difficult to face from personal experience, so I can freely speak on this. Considering my mother chose my abusive father over all 5 of her children, I definitely wanted to know more on the topic.

You automatically feel like you are not good enough…worthless. When I lived in a world that saw a person as their other half, I never felt whole. Growing up in the South, many believe that if you are not married by a certain age, there must be something wrong with you. As if you are broken…ineffective until you "find your other half." One day I was forced to face all of the pain, shortly after my perspective had changed. I now see I live in a society that knows you have to be whole before being with another person who is already whole. Seeing yourself as half will force you to adopt the I need another person principle. Instead of allowing another individual to be a want…a bonus to your life. Companionship is human nature, but what is the rush to have it? And what are you sacrificing for it? Nowadays, it has become more and more common to be single. The problem is most people struggle with what to do. How to get a sense of freedom.

People often think just take time and you will naturally heal and renew. As if it is the type of physical scar that just needs a proper length of time to blend back in. What I am noticing is when those people get back in a relationship before they are healed and ready…they either take baggage from their past relationship into the new one, seek someone similar to their ex, if not worse, or sacrificing their standards...aka settling just to have a hot body lying next to you. Those people looked over their internal injuries. In my experience, I've seen how much unhealed internal damage has done to people over time. Me included. I, too, have made the mistake of staying with someone longer than I should have just to avoid my abandonment issues with lack of self-love. Once upon a time, I was always involved with someone. Jumping from relationship to relationship to avoid my pain and insecurities. Over time, avoidance has detrimental effects for yourself and loved ones. The cure for feeling lonely is to face being alone. Eventually, you will see that the person you choose to be with reflects yourself. Sometimes you have to go through those relationships that are lessons, they only improve your self-awareness. If you grew from it. The person you are choosing to be with, what do they reveal about your character? Maybe it is just me, but wouldn't you want to improve the person you are first to welcome the type of partner you deserve? If you decide you need one at all.

Perhaps the advice given over the years is assumption based. We talk about loving ourselves but never how to love ourselves. We talk about the importance of being single after a relationship but not how to be single or what to do with that time. We talk about forgiveness with others, and yet can't see the importance of forgiving ourselves. Don't be bitter...be better. Rejection is redirection. Love is a verb and worth the commitment. Follow my journey from feeling like half to being whole. Gratitude is my new attitude because I came out on the other side of things.

CHAPTER 1

Mirror Mirror (Judgments and Reflections)

Mirror, mirror on the wall.
How do I see myself overall?

When no one is around, and no one can see.
What vision do I secretly believe?

Did I make the memories in my life?
Or did they make me?

What did my inner child want me to be?
No matter what, having self-love is the key.

As you, I am a perfectly imperfect human being.
Sometimes things aren't as they seem.

Once you accept your flaws, you'll know what I mean.
Life…is…but…a…dream.

"*The woman you are becoming will cost you people, relationships, spaces, and material things. Choose her over everything.*" – Arpita Kundu

Taking away judgment and processing reflections are key to self-awareness.

We keep ourselves prisoner to the surroundings of our minds.

Our minds are set up to work against us by judging, labeling, comparing, and criticizing. This is a negativity bias, meaning our minds are naturally set up to work against us. Your brain lives in survival mode of fight or flight and continues to watch for any dangers that may be a threat. We naturally live in an egoic state. The only way your ego survives is by working against you through thoughts. Believing the thoughts that exist over time makes you a prisoner of the mind. To experience true joy, you have to consciously work against your own mind. If that sounds difficult, then you understand exactly what that might entail.

Think of it this way. You have your subconscious, which is the majority of your brain, and your conscious is just 1 out of the 8 pizza slices. Your subconscious is like a computer system in your brain that records all the events in your life since the third trimester of you being in your mother's womb. Which means our solutions for any event comes from information already stored. Since it is already in the system, no new information is needed to come up with the best data/solution. If there are 5 levels (1.0, 2.0, 3.0, etc.), then you must take in new experiences and learn new information to upgrade your system. If not, it stays at 1.0 in all things you do. Your subconscious is all your habits on repeat. To break those habits, you have to try to live consciously. You do this by being mindful of everything you do; only then can see new things and you question things more to come up with a better solution. To be mindful, you must be present, be in the moment, take in everything about what you are doing. For example, if you are eating your lunch, eliminate the multitasking and do only that...eat. Direct all of your attention to eating and focus only on it. This time do it in its entirety. You can do this by taking in the smell, the individual ingredients that make up the taste, the sound it makes while chewing, the texture, the noises it makes when breaking pieces apart. By doing this with everything throughout the day, you are living mindfully in a conscious state becoming more and self-aware. Without self-awareness, you will believe everything your mind tells you about yourself.

Judgments.

It is overwhelming to have negative thoughts on repeat throughout the day and not be aware of them. Once you become self-aware, the door to allowance opens. What you resist eventually persists. Once you stop resisting and allow things to be, you realize all of your suffering is created in your mind. Accepting what is and letting go of the rest allows resistance to fall away.

Giving yourself a choice with the freedom to respond instead of reacting. This is the foundation of a mindful life. Just remember this:

3 Simple Steps:

Release judgment.

Accept what is.

React with intention.

Simple.

"Life is 10% what happens to you and 90% how you handle it." We can't change our past; we can't change people's actions and we also can't change what is bound to happen. What we can do is always react and handle every situation to the best of our ability. Every single day, hour, minute, and second of our lives, each and every one of us has the choice regarding what type of attitude we want to have in that second, minute, hour, or day.

We all have a story. An illusion of what happened in the past. I love calling it just that, a "story." Anything other than that would make it true with society-based labels attached.

Life is full of choices and sometimes making one wrong decision can change the fate of your destiny. I guess the saying that you can either learn from other people's mistakes or repeat them is an understatement. I made a conscious effort to become nothing like the ways of my father. I lived my life doing the opposite things I saw him do. I didn't foresee myself triggering the traits of my mother from a life choice she made. Maybe because I cast judgment. Unlike her, I eventually eliminated the judgments and reflected. Only through reflection, I saw the possible outcomes and learned from the mistakes of others. It all came down to me making a choice she was never able to make. I chose my son then left and every decision after that got easier.

As I sat in the chair across from my therapist, I'll never forget what she said. "Malissa, your mom will never be able to accept nor support your decision because she was never strong enough to do it." I also remember calling bullshit. I can be hardheaded that way. Well, turns out she was right. Who would have ever thought the day would come where I have to choose myself or my parents? The moment I chose myself is the moment I discovered what love truly was. Their decisions had nothing to do with me. It wasn't about me. I make it about myself when I

am stuck inside my mind, I make it about me.

Truth is, after working on myself a lot, I made the 4 agreements promise from the book to myself:

1. Be impeccable with my word.
2. Don't take anything personally
3. Don't make assumptions.
4. Always do my best.

By doing this, you are forced to figure out the root of the problem and live in the solution. Upon doing this, I discovered they had no clue what love was or is and since they didn't know what it was, this meant they never loved themselves, and if they didn't love themselves or knew what it was for that matter, they were incapable of loving me or my siblings. I would like to believe that their self-absorption throughout my life was them constantly chasing it. That their constant search in getting their worth through external materialistic things lead them to base love off constant things for self which ultimately made them selfish.

So how do I give myself self-love without taking it too far and becoming absorbed in myself? Do I look at doing this in moderation or situational based? Love, so many meanings and ways of expressing it. Without a doubt, for me love is a verb. This keeps it clearly defined. I used to believe that if someone said it …they meant it. You can see where the confusions came in. Maybe in their own way of thinking they know what it was, they did. After reading the 5 languages of love, I realized people do not give and receive love in the same way. Sometimes people are not feeling loved because you are not speaking their love language. We automatically assume the way we want to be loved is how others want to be loved as well.

That looks like two people who speak different languages trying to communicate.

Knowing your love language along with the other person you want to show love to love language, can change the entire dynamic of the relationship.

Here are the 5 languages of love, we all have one or possibly even two ways we receive love:

1. Words of Affirmation
2. Quality Time
3. Receiving Gifts
4. Acts of Service
5. Physical Touch

Thinking back to your childhood, how did your parents make you feel loved. This will be your first instinct.

Have you been hurt in the past? What hurt the most? Maybe the person who hurt you was clueless about love making them clueless that love languages exist.

Although not knowing that doesn't excuse what we can all do. The simplicity in asking your loved one's questions such as:

When do they feel loved the most?

What makes them smile or feel special?

This is communication 101 people and takes a matter of seconds.

Sometimes life gets overly complicated and you have to fill your tank before you feel burnt out, causing you to run on fumes. Love is a choice and a feeling. Being self-aware by showing your love through action ensures love is coming from a genuine place.

Self-awareness makes you not just aware of yourself. Eventually, you become aware of others and learn that we all want and need the same things.

If you are not consciously aware of this, your story can keep you mentally stuck into your constant wants disguised as needs for instant gratification. Which means your need for externally instant gratification indicates that you lack self-love. You believe this way of acting to be lovingly because of the repeat story playing in your head. The constant replay forces you to believe it to be true. It doesn't have to always be our personal story; it can be the story of your environment. Sometimes the stories from the people around us are based on the choices they made, if not self-aware, other people's stories can indirectly predetermine our next path without us knowing. This is often called generational curses.

To understand how I came to my situation, let's start with some of my background.

Once you overcome negatively judging yourself, your self-esteem increases.

As previously mentioned, your mind is set up to work against you. Once you overcome negatively judging yourself, your self-esteem will increase. Most people fear negative judgment from others. We spend so much time wondering what other people think of us we overlook our personal judgment upon ourselves.

This consistent self-judgment of ourselves eventually causes a drop in self-esteem. Once you are in this state of mind, you have to work through it as soon as possible.

Because emotionally continuing to feel that way leads to mental health issues such as anxiety and depression. With mental health issues such as these, you no longer have control over your own mind preventing you from doing simple day to day activities and eventually causing isolation. Once the negative self-judgment stops, your self-esteem increases leading to a life of more fulfillment.

How to Stop negative self-judgment.

Negatively judging yourself has become a habit from your subconscious, it is programmed and used daily. So how do we stop that?

"Your beliefs become your thoughts,
Your thoughts become your words,
Your words become your actions,
Your actions become your habits,
Your habits become your values,
Your values become your destiny."

— Gandhi

We have these automatic thoughts that run on repeat every second of the day. To take back control of your mind, you have to question where these thoughts come from. Where else besides your beliefs. The same beliefs you developed through your earlier experiences in life. Until now, there was no reason to question those beliefs. The good news is, there is enough power within you to change all of this because when we know better, we do better. Let's get started with some tips to stop negative self-judgment and become one step closer to increasing our self-esteem:

- Pay attention to more of your negative thoughts and words. You have to become the watcher of your thoughts. Question what you must have been thinking to say negative things. Take a breath before responding and go against what you initially would have said. See the positive solutions consciously to everything instead of the negative automatic ones through self-defeating beliefs. Become your biggest cheerleader instead of your biggest self-critic. Because you must.

- Be mindful in all that you do. Everyone knows how to be mindful, we learned so when we were children. Start with the basics, your senses. See, smell, hear, feel, and sometimes taste. That's the secret ingredient to being present. A refresher from earlier. To be mindful of what you are doing, you cannot multitask. For example, if you are going to eat...only eat. Focus on the taste of what you are eating down to the individual ingredients. The texture and the sound it makes whenever you chew. The smell, how does it smell to you. Enjoy that moment for what it is. Nothing else matters but eating in that moment. Congratulations, that is how you become present through mindfulness and you just did that.

- Stop running on the hamster wheel of assumptions. One negative outcome from a situation in your life does not equate to you being stupid or a failure in general. Who told you that you are your negative experiences? No one, you assumed this through overgeneralizing. Focus on your successes in life, write them all down and focus on positive outcomes and know to get to the positive outcomes it sometimes has to be via a lesson from the failures. It is all a part of growth not a definition of who you are as a person.

- Focus on Facts over Feelings. Just because you feel sad doesn't mean you are, maybe you are just tired, sleepy, or dehydrated. Challenge why you are feeling and thinking negative things that do not add up to your situation. There are no facts to support your conclusions and maybe you only lack data.
- Do you believe people when they give you a compliment? Why is it we are more likely to believe the negative things people say about us over the positives? STOP this immediately and accept the compliments people give you with only gratitude. Anything other than that will be negative self-judgment. And of course, you don't want the person giving the compliments to feel rejection from your comment. It's not always about you.
- Affirmations. Say your affirmations in the mirror daily until you can only focus on the positive things about your life. Build it into a daily habit for 30 days straight. If you miss a day, start over. Mirror work allows you to face the truth about yourself.
- Love every single thing about yourself. We are all imperfectly perfect human beings. Our imperfections give us our gifts. Be

gentle with yourself and look into that same mirror and love on each body part you for some reason do not like.

- Be your own best friend. Give yourself the same advice you would give your best friend. Put your best friend in your situation and think about what you would tell them if the roles were reversed.
- One of my favorites is listening to Focus Music like Binaural Beats for Concentration. We all have highs and lows throughout our lives. Surfing the lows better can be tricky. Our minds are set up to work against us, especially depending on the information downloaded into your system over time. I like to override the bullshit…the spam. I do this by constantly telling my mind what to focus on. I have my headphones on me at all times. Whether grocery shopping or reading…anytime I know I am feeling some type of way I like to override that information to get things done. This is me being positive by constantly listening to positive things or focus music.

It is important to know, "you don't just wake up and become the butterfly, growth is a process and well worth the wait." -Rupi Kaur

Reasons You Should Never Judge Other People

Some people judge other people without ever realizing and then you have those people who absolutely love it. It is easier to focus on other people's shit over our own. Doing so gives you that temporary boost in self-esteem, it is a quick fix. No judgment. We all have been there. I remember this saying from elementary school, "when you point your finger at someone else's imperfections, you have 3 pointing back at you for a reason. It is hard to notice our own mistakes, and easy to point out someone else when none of us have the right to judge. It is time to replace this self-defeating habit and here is why:

1. You don't have enough data in your brain about the person to make a calculated decision. Your decision about them is based on the information in your personal mind cloud. Assumption based. We all have a story, just as I don't know yours, you do not know mine. Focus on facts over feelings. If you can help, then help and if not, then let it go.

2. We all have different backgrounds, experiences, education, preferences. If we all were the same, then things could get boring quickly or not depending on your preferences of things. I remember being a die-hard Christian back in the day and in my attempt to help people, I projected judgment and assumed that because of my beliefs their beliefs were wrong. Now I know how important it is to seek understanding from another human being and leave the judgment behind. Instead, question what is going on with yourself to feel the need to judge someone else. Redirect that focus back onto yourself in a healthy, loving way. We are all created differently and that is okay.

3. Even perfectionists eventually learn the hard way that no one is perfect. We all make mistakes, who gave you the authority to criticize someone else as if you have all the answers. Diminish the ego by flirting with the possibility of being wrong sometimes.

4. Treat others the way you would want to be treated.

It only takes seconds to destroy a relationship by voicing misplaced judgments from ourselves to others. Getting back to the strong relationship you once had with this person that took time for trust to build is gone and will take so much longer to get back if you ever do. Think about that before judging.

5. What do you do when you have a coworker you don't like but have to deal with anyway…you tolerate. LOL. Accept that you will run across people in life completely different than you. Seek to understand and if you still don't understand, that is okay, now would be a good time to incorporate tolerance. Focus on the problems you have within your own life instead because the more we understand ourselves, the more tolerance we have for what we see in others.

6. Appearances can be misleading. I can vouch for this. Although the world always saw me as this beautiful woman with her shit together and couldn't have a problem in the world because I didn't look like I did. I would look into the mirror and for a while and only see a broken little girl with so much pain on the inside. I needed compassion and got judgments. And then there are people in this world worth a lot financially, their appearance looks like they live in poverty, and they give so much of themselves to helping others. You also have people who look like a million bucks and have only a few bucks to their name. Appearances have a reputation for being deceptive.

7. Respect for yourself and others is important. Once you respect yourself, it is easier to respect others and once you respect others, you will have no problem with respecting someone you consider an enemy. Respecting your enemies is the quickest way to grow. Think about it this way. "He who angers you controls you" – Elizabeth Kenny. Take back your control by figuring out why you really got angry. Words from an enemy cannot hurt you unless you believe what they are saying to be true. It always comes back to how you feel about yourself…weird, huh. BOUNDARIES.

8. What you do, and how you do it does not align with who you are. How do you define yourself? Cliff-notes version, whatever you are judging in others or gets you bent out of shape with others, only does this because secretly, that is how you see yourself when you look into the mirror. Stop being so judgmental. No worries, because once we are done, the mirror will be your best friend instead of the enemy you used to run from.

Self-Reflection.

When you think about self-reflection, what comes to mind? Personal reflection is the first step in taking responsibility for your life. It is taking the time out to think about, meditate, and evaluate the reason behind your thoughts, behaviors, attitudes, desires, and motivations. An easy way I dive into all my thoughts is by journaling. Putting the problem into physical form by thinking it out on paper for a solution. Self-reflection not only helps you to see the bigger perspective but the details between. For example: Where are you headed? Are you happy with the direction you are moving in? And are you able to make the proper adjustments along the way? That is seeing things from a big perspective. A small perspective gives you the allowance to evaluate your reaction to particular events and circumstances.

"Reflection is a deeper form of learning that allows us to retain every aspect of any experience, be it personal or professional — why something took place, what the impact was, whether it should happen again — as opposed to just remembering that it happened. It's about tapping into every aspect of the experience, clarifying our thinking, and homing in on what really matters to us."

— Geil Browning, Ph.D.,

Knowing thyself is a difficult unnatural thing to do for most. It will take you having a different perspective, open to possibilities, discipline, and being intentional in your pursuit. What makes this a valuable practice is we live in a life full of chaos, you have to learn to stop what's going around you and redirect your attention onto yourself.

A life without personal reflection causes you to move robotically throughout life. Just moving from one thing to the next without pausing to think about circumstances or evaluate new solutions. How else will you know what is working well and what is not. Without stopping to analyze things, it becomes easier to get stuck. Before I started self-reflection, I was working at a job I didn't like and tolerating relationship bullshit longer than I should have. You eventually feel as if you are running in circles on a hamster wheel. Things aren't going well within your life, but it remains easier to just continue on with the process of things even though they are not good. Survival instead of thriving in life. We feel like we are going insane from doing the same things repeatedly and expecting different results.

Even though taking time out for personal reflection can be challenging and difficult, the benefits outweigh any negative aspect. Therefore, we should all make time for it. Here are a few:

It gives you a different perspective.

The dictionary's definition of emotions is to have a natural instinctive state of mind deriving from one's circumstances, mood, or relationships with others. Emotions have determined how people feel. What if what you perceive to be your emotions is really just clouding your judgment on what is going on. This can cause you to lose sight on things through a distorted way of believing it to be. Personal reflection allows you to ignore the unimportant things and focus on processing events in your life the correct way to give you clarity.

It allows you to be proactive instead of reactive. When our emotions go unchecked, we react to whatever situation comes our way. In those moments, we lack control, we later regret what was said in a reactive state of mind. Yes, taking time for self-reflection can be difficult. It is challenging when you take the time needed to step back and reflect on what truly matters. Self-reflection has a numerous amount of wonderful benefits, which makes it worth the time and effort put into it for everyone.

Self-reflection allows you to take a breath in that moment to think about the consequences of our actions and respond instead of reacting.

It encourages knowledge and understanding by evaluating and processing the things we experienced. Without it, there is no way to gain a deeper understanding of our own lives. Self-Reflection gives you back control over your life by gaining an understanding of the meaning of our circumstances, emotions, and motivations. This leads to a healthier lifestyle.

What we see in others reflects ourselves.

In an attempt not to get too spiritual with the truth of such a strong statement, I would like for you to ponder on this for a moment without overthinking. As we discussed earlier, the reason certain things about other people get you so upset is because your mind and body are reacting to what is within you. Same thing different perspective, *"More often than not, the things we detest and judge in others are a reflection of the things we cannot accept about ourselves'* -Iyanla Vanzant. This is one of the most enlightening spiritual lessons we will come across. Remember when I talked about my journey in trying to learn about others so that I cannot be so upset with the things they do in the future, but come to find out I was actually the problem? Yea, it was an ah-ha moment for me as well.

Why is it that everyone you meet is your mirror?

We understand ourselves better through the company we keep and the relationships we encounter. Our brains, which is our own personal software system that has recorded only the experiences within our lives, knows how to respond to our body through emotions previously experienced. Basically, when we get upset with others, we can only be triggered by something we have experienced ourselves. This leads to us judging ourselves and criticizing the same characteristics within ourselves. This goes back to our earlier example of pointing a blaming finger at someone with one finger pointing at the person being blamed and three pointing back at ourselves.

It is not about that person; it is about us. Let's make it about us. Think of it this way, having certain characteristics in another individual triggering a negative reaction within means it is coming up within yourself because it is ready to be healed. So, the next time you are emotionally triggered by someone else, just know this is a part of the growth process and you have just learned something new about yourself to get ahead in a positive way instead of feeling self-defeated or angry. Usually, when this happens, it is a representative of issues from your past that have gone unresolved. I learned the reason I was constantly attracting people who betray me in close relationships is because at the time I haven't dealt with my parental abandonment issues from my past. The manifestation I was seeing was the belief I could trust no one with my feelings. Another reason for this manifestation could also be that you have a constant need to prove to others that you *are "right."* Which means you will constantly attract people who also want to convince you to see life from their perspective. Being attracted to controlling people also can mean you have control issues within yourself that you strongly dislike.

The people we meet within our lives are showing up not by coincidence, they come at a time we need to reflect on the things we need to heal within. These people are showing you who you are and giving you a chance to learn and love certain qualities within. Consider these people to be your greatest teachers in life.

What to do when you find yourself in a situation that triggers you?

Take a breath and start by asking yourself certain questions for better insight: Have you forgiven yourself? Do you love yourself? If you are easily triggered…you probably don't. Because one of the most effective ways to disengage from negative interactions to forgive yourself. Depending on how much you love and accept yourself is the same amount you can give to others. If you do not love and accept yourself, then chances are you do not love and accept others for who they are. You cannot give something you do not have within to give. Learning from your relationships is the key. Once you learn, you will make it a habit to discover that you can observe the actions of other's negativity without judgment or the involvement within their perceived drama. If the person is abusive, then it is wise to avoid them entirely. Embrace to lessons fully, forgive yourself, and forgive that person.

On a positive note, just like you can see the undesirable behaviors in another person also within you. You can see the desirable behaviors within someone else that is also within you. When we choose thoughts of positivity, we tend to live in a positive loving world. Continuing to keep our light bright and focusing on it, will bring out the light within others.

- **Mind**- Do you feel coherent, connected with, and mentally tested?
- **Body**- Does your body feel sound, sustained, and solid?
- **Soul**- Do you feel settled and associated with your general surroundings?

- **Work**- Do you feel intrigued by and satisfied by your work?
- **Play**- Do you feel euphoric? Is it safe to say that you are taking part in exercises that bring you satisfaction?
- **Love**- Do you feel good about the connections throughout your life?

By focusing on these 6 things you are eliminating judgments, forcing reflection and strengthening your self-awareness. Congratulations, this is your first commitment to self.

CHAPTER 2

A Commitment to Me, Myself, and I (Forgiveness)

"Sometimes trying to save others can cost you yourself, that is definitely not worth it."

Letter to my Mother:

Dear Mom,

I know you did the best you could with what you had, that is what I will continue to tell myself, it helps me empathize with you as a woman. There isn't anything that can change the unconditional love I have for you as my mother. For me, everything changed when I learned you didn't love yourself, at that moment, I stopped taking it personally that the two of you didn't know how to love any of us. I often wonder what a Queen means to you. Women have superpowers you never told me about. Maybe you didn't know, which would make sense because I never saw you use yours. Due to your lack of self-love, our relationship was strained. How can you love me when you do not love yourself or believe the same?

I watched the damage being done to you slowly over time by the only father I knew. Now you have permanent damage, and I will never genuinely know you, but that is why I want to make sure everyone else do believe. I know you think it sounds crazy to seek help for things unseen. Mental Health is a huge problem and affects more than just me. My image was blurry, and after getting self-awareness now, I can see myself. Mental Health is generational and developed in a toxic environment. You had four girls, one boy, and none of us was prepared properly. And to this day, you still only see from your perspective, love for the man who knowingly did this to you. Continuing to defend him as if this is all make-believe. I'm convinced you'll continue to choose him over your flesh, your seeds. I want to shake you to wake you because I know you're mentally in a dream. You reached all the breaking points most women would up and leave. Ignoring our cries for help, the pain that is self-medicated and too big to bear. Growing up wanting to die because no one seemed to care. I know you see us physically and want to only believe that we are just fine, but on the inside, we hide what feels like distorted minds. I grew up thinking women were not important. You made me believe that the female voice didn't matter. Thank God for my aunts. Or else I'd still believe we have nothing to gain. Instead of a 50/50 partnership, I guess you questioned your worth and became mentally crippled to your pain. I was confused because it seemed like you were the only one who thought you couldn't do what you are the only one who did.

As leaders, men may have the power, but women are more powerful.

I remember wanting to be a boy, thinking that was the only way to gain strength. Did you ever ask yourself the important questions or did it all really just remain on the surface? It seemed like you'd rather accept the truth in the lie and fight the facts to keep your feelings from the thought of pain.

I forgive you both.

I officially divorced my parents to keep my sanity intact and then I married myself because…

"Without commitment nothing different happens." – T.D. Jakes

What does a commitment to yourself look like for you? How often do you stop to see how you are doing? Where there is pain or you are being triggered, or even hurt, do you go through the steps of stopping to ask how you are doing? As human beings we have a habit of turning to our vice, blaming, or numbing out. We have a habit of diverting our way to external factors. It only takes a few basic actions of giving the self-love we give to others to ourselves. Learn to check in on yourself.

In the past, I had a habit of staying busy. In hindsight, I now see it was another method to avoid the pain. I felt silly for still feeling a certain way about a situation that was done with and felt it was more productive to avoid the lingering effects and stay busy. I ended up putting myself into depression. Avoidance of things, anything, eventually lead to depression. I've learned to stop and give myself an assessment via meditation, journaling, and sometimes mirror talk. I learned the hard way that by not making an inquiry every now and then of yourself is another way of avoiding something temporality.

We've all heard the saying, give yourself the advice you would give your best friend. The things we do for others in their time of need are the things we want done for ourselves. So, do those things for yourself. Realize that self-love is committing to yourself first. Society sometimes paints this out to be selfish. Far from being selfish. The harsh reality is, you cannot pour from an empty cup.

To get it in its entirety, you must marry yourself, and fully commit to the marriage as you would if it was another person involved, such as a husband or wife. Your commitment to yourself has to be way bigger than anything you desire from another individual. The things you want or feel you need from another individual are the things lacking within yourself. It is very important for you to give that to yourself first. Growing up, I was taught the opposite, so I did not learn this until recently within my adult life. I've come a long way. Guess what? If I could do it, then so can you.

I've learned it is important to take care of yourself first whenever you are feeling emotionally charged. Things work out for the best in all areas of your life when you simply stop what you are doing and ask yourself a few questions. This helps you to navigate life with authenticity, clarity, and peace instead of moving throughout your day emotionally frustrated, stressed out, or hurt.

So, what are these self-evaluating questions to ask when feeling triggered or a little unsettled?

How are you feeling?

What sensations are your body having from feeling this way? What was the thought that caused this reaction?

Write down these thoughts and feelings.

Then ask you're the following about it:

What facts make this true? Take a breath and process it.

What reactions am I having from this?

Why?

What can I learn from this whether it is positive or negative?

What makes this true?

What are some specific examples of this?

By now, you should have processed this in its entirety and realized judgment created the charge of emotions. Curiously asking questions can defuse those emotional charges. This is you taking charge and committing to yourself.

That little girl within needed me to commit to her for personal growth and I can never tell her no in her pursuit to self-awareness, she needs to be seen and heard. Although she may have been abandoned by everyone else, I have to show her that this marriage is a lifetime commitment. Showing her is the unconditional love, committing to myself is the marriage, taking responsibility of my life is the finances, and personal growth is the sex.

I walked around with a smile on my face, but with so much pain and frustration on the inside. Constantly in a pursuit to fix others to make me better. My logic was obviously flawed. I had it wrong. Seems silly saying it. Maybe that was me trying to control others to be better so I can feel comfortable being around them. Seems like a mixture of selfishness, judgment, and control. It is the opposite, work on yourself and only yourself if you genuinely want an improvement in your relationships. You can offer more to others and yourself. Much better that way. Healthier, freer, loving, joyful perspective to have. I have become obsessed with personal growth. We all know what it takes to get results for physical health, time to learn and improve your mental health as well. I'm always in the mirror checking myself, if I don't, who else will. It is my responsibility alone. Be your own coach and take charge of your life.

I've been chasing self-growth my entire life, a few years ago, I finally got in a relationship with it and I'm happy to say I'm falling in love with myself. Your commitment to yourself will be the practice you need for your future life partner. You both will be grateful for it.

I've had the pleasure of being with myself while depressed, anxious, in pain, and in the times of joy. I remember when I use to hate myself, it showed in my toxic actions. I stood by myself when no one else did, even in the times I wanted to end it all. I survived it all here I stand still loving myself.

It almost takes the shape of narcissistically loving yourself. It is a different type of love you have to be and give, almost like you need to learn what love is and how you love for the first time. You need patience, communication, acceptance, and the ability to be gentle with yourself. When getting frustrated, remember to ask yourself those questions. After all, we cannot leave ourselves for too long whenever frustrated because your whole objective is to be the one, we want to come home to.

Self-Care. To get the things you want from yourself, you must take care of yourself.

Write down some things you usually do to take care of yourself. A list of the things you do for self-care. It can be the simple things in life you like to do for yourself that takes little effort, time, or money. It can be something to enhance your physical appearances such as mani/pedi, spiritually by getting out in nature, etc. On my journey, I realized that the things I loved doing as a child are the very same things that feed my soul present day.

Here is a great list to get started with:

10 Commandments for a Commitment to Yourself.

1. Stop 'People Pleasing," don't compromise your happiness for the sake of pleasing someone else. We are all imperfectly perfect different human beings. It is in our individuality that give us characteristics of who we are. Stop judging that difference and embrace. "Be who you are and say what you feel, because those who mind don't matter, and those who matter don't mind." – Bernard M. Baruch

2. Responsibility breeds empowerment. Take charge of your life by being responsible for everything that happens in it. Do you base the outcome of the things that happen in your life on external things or would you say they are the results to the decisions you made? What was your response? Whatever it was, this shows you your perspective. To become more conscious, you have to look at things in an objective way. Are you being the victim by placing blame or are you empowering yourself with responsibility? To be in control of the things that happen in your outside world, you have to take complete responsibility.

3. Realize that making mistakes is a part of life. To grow or get better, mistakes have to be made. Think about it; everything in life requires you to fail, so there is no need to avoid it. Instead, embrace failure and be willing to fail as much and as fast as possible for continued growth. A successful person is never afraid to fail.

4. No is a full sentence, enforce your boundaries and learn to say it more often. Yes, people often feel pressured by friends to do the things they have no interest in doing. When you say no to those things, this shows you have discipline and personal boundaries, which is very important in the commitment

process to yourself for choosing you more. It takes some getting used to using the word no if it is normally unfamiliar for you, but people will respect you more for using it.

5. What is done is done, stop worrying about the choices you've made in the past. The choices you made in your life up to this point were made based on your personal values and boundaries. You either are the type of person who stands your ground and makes all your decisions based off of the ones you have or the type of person who never took the time out to figure out what your values and boundaries are, which would explain the constant lack of control you feel in your life. Becoming more self-aware takes away the anxiety and depression you would have experienced in the long term. Knowing thyself helps you learn to accept what is and trust yourself enough to let go of the rest.

6. Being gentle with yourself helps to accept what is.

Be gently by consciously accepting what you consider your successes as well as your failures. Without acceptance, it is hard to develop into that humble character I know you are. You have to actively accept what comes your way win, lose, or draw, and only from there allows you to change and improve.

7. Actively show gratitude. Make it a daily habit of starting your day by writing down at least 3 things you are grateful for. The awareness comes when it becomes 3 different things daily.

A friend who was there for me in a time of need once told me that everyone has problems and your problems are not as bad as they seem in your head. If there was a circle of people each holding a piece of paper with their biggest problem written down with a hat in the middle and everyone was instructed to drop their piece of paper in the hat. Then wait for the person who instructed this to shake up the hat full of problems and everyone pull out a piece of paper from the hat randomly. The catch is that the new piece of paper with a different problem on it, now has to be accepted as theirs. Well, everyone would want their original problem back in realizing it isn't as bad as they thought compared to someone else. It doesn't matter how bad your present-day situation is, someone will always be dealing with something worse. Showing gratitude in written form is a constant reminder of this and eliminates your perspective over time.

8. We are all imperfect human beings, the people striving to be perfectionists still haven't learned this. It is only when you accept your flaws, they lose the power to be used against you. Without self-acceptance, there will be a lack of genuine growth.

9. Rejection is redirection, embrace it.

Release expectations of the outcomes in your life beyond your control. It is often hard for people, including myself, to detach your internal self from the external rejection. Once you stop giving rejection the value it doesn't deserve, it loses its power over you and you can now redirect your attention and actions.

10. Remember, there is a light at the end of the tunnel, whether you are dealing with good times or bad, the constant is you will continue to face it. The tunnel symbolizes you having to go through it to see the light at the end. We are always either about to go through something going through something, or

just getting out of something. Tackle what you can, accept what you cannot, and let go of everything else.

Forgiveness.

We have been taught for so long on different ways to forgive others, have you ever considered that maybe the guilt is still there because you have yet to forgive yourself?

You often hear people say how important it is to forgive yourself if you ever want to have peace within and move forward with your life. How does one go about on doing this? How do you get the understanding or compassion or kindness, or empathy from within to forgive yourself? First, know that forgiveness is a choice. Whether you view the "unforgivable situation" as something minor or major you will need to take the same steps each time to forgive. As the imperfect human beings that we are, we will all make mistakes in life. You will feel pain regardless, it is the symptom to the problem and an indication to yourself that something is wrong. Instead of avoiding the pain, realize to forgive yourself and move on you must feel the pain. Here are tips on how to forgive yourself and work through the pain instead of around it:

1. Process the emotions you feel. To process the emotions, you feel, you must first acknowledge them. Welcome those emotions from your triggers, it is the only way to accept what is and move forward.

2. Verbally acknowledge the mistake in front of a mirror. To shut off the hamster wheel in your mind, acknowledge the mistake out loud and it helps with acceptance doing this in front of a mirror. Instead of a repeat made-up story in your

head, when you say it out loud, you are releasing the burdens you feel and recreate that story in your mind to what you know to be true with an everlasting imprint from acknowledgment of the consequences and actions.

3. Shift your perspective of what you believe a mistake to be. Instead of dwelling on what you see as being negative in it, make it something you can learn from for the better. Instead of beating yourself up constantly as if you did something wrong, understand that without that mistake, you could not learn something new in your own personal growth. We have learned better from mistakes since we were children. After taking actions to do things like touch the hot stove, we realize the consequences are a burnt hand. Between the action, consequence, and your memorable reaction, I think it is safe to say you treat stoves completely differently now. This same analogy applies to the mistakes we make in life. Remind yourself daily you are doing the best you can with the tools, resources, and knowledge you have.

4. It is okay to deal with the process of things at a later date and time, as long as you are not just ignoring or numbing. To press pause, you have to tell yourself and visualize the process of what putting it on hold may look like. Whether you say it out loud as you visualize yourself putting it in a safe deposit box for later withdrawal.

5. Look into a mirror and converse with your inner critic. Writing down your feelings from your inner critic can help you to develop understanding and self-compassion. May sound silly but journaling the conversation between you and your inner critic can help you figure out how you are self-sabotaging yourself through negative thought patterns, which

ultimately interferes with forgiveness of oneself. After journaling the dialogue, it would be a good idea to write down as many of your strengths and skills you have to help your confidence so you can stop feeling down about the mistake.

6. Acknowledge when you are being self-critical. As discussed earlier on, our minds are set up to work against us, which makes us our own worse critics. Notice more of when you are doing this, write it down and work through the process.

7. Replace the negative messages of your inner critic with something positive, like daily affirmations. Instead of trying to figure out which negative thoughts you are having, listen to positive affirmations to discredit it. Or you can take a piece of paper and write down all the critical things being said on one side and on the other side, discredit the critic with self-compassionate responses.

8. Be very specific about what you want. If this involves another person, then figure the best way to go about making amends. Doing this helps with forgiving ourselves as well. Sometimes saying sorry isn't enough.

9. What advice would you give someone else who is in the same situation? We can often give good advice to others but cannot see the situation for what it is when it is our own. The simple solution would be to visually put someone else in your situation and take the advice you would have given them as your own.

10. It is time to break the tape recorder being played on repeat. Processing a mistake and playing it on repeat are two different things. The natural thing we all do as human beings is to spend time and energy playing our mistakes on repeat in your minds.

The processing on your mistake is important and one of the key elements that lead to forgiveness. Try interrupting that thought pattern with a positive action such as a few deep breaths, going for a walk in nature, or listening to something positive.

11. Have compassion with yourself. To have compassion for yourself, you have to be gentle and kind with yourself.
12. Getting professional help isn't a weakness, it is a strength. If all else fails, then it is time to seek outside help for inside help. Professionals always have healthier ways of processing mistakes.

When you have underlying guilt, shame, anger, sadness, or other negative feelings you are experiencing with forgiveness is the key to the healing process to move on. Once you acknowledge your feelings, put a name to it verbally or visually, it becomes easier to accept and once you accept, you realize that mistakes are a part of life and are inevitable. We all make mistakes, but not all of us get a chance to move forward in a healthy way. Moving forward gives you freedom.

A quick reminder is the 4 R's to Self-Forgiveness

- Responsibility
- Remorse
- Restoration
- Renewal.

CHAPTER 3

Fit and Lit (Mental vs Physical Wellness)

"Change the mind, and the body will follow. Change the spirit, and reality will shift."

I remember looking in the mirror and having so many negative thoughts on replay about my body image. I was about to head out and meet a few friends.

I changed my outfit maybe 4 or 5 times, which caused me to be late. Rushing to get there, I felt like my hair was all over the place and I needed a little makeup. Here I am on my way to have a good time and feeling so down because I was consumed in my appearance. As soon as I arrived, the first thing one of my friends said is how I always look so effortless, beautiful and how annoying that is. WOW! You have no idea how much that meant. I get we are our own worse critics, but why? I was actively in the gym, and although I thought I could stand to go a little more, I looked amazingly fit to others. At that moment, I knew I had an unresolved mental issue I have yet to deal with. I looked amazing and had been told so everywhere I went. Don't get me wrong, I knew this to be true, just questioned it more often then I should have. It would be easy to blame things on my emotionally abusive ex, but what good would that do when the truth was, I couldn't see myself. At that moment, I knew it would take more than being physically fit, I needed to get lit mentally, emotionally, and spiritually as well to see things for what they truly are consistently.

The World Health Organization (WHO) defines mental health as the state of wellbeing where every individual realizes his or her own potential, manages the normal stresses of life, works productively and fruitfully, and can contribute to her or his community. You have optimal mental health; your mental function is consistently at a state of successful performance. Which means you are engaged in productive activities, fulfilling relationships with other people, and you can adapt well to change. To have a healthy well-being with family and interpersonal relationships, and be at a state of mind to want to contribute to the community or society, then mental health is essential. Constantly having alterations in emotions by your thinking, mood, and behavior are all associated with distress from impaired functioning. Mental disorders contribute to a host of problems that lead to pain, disability, or death.

Mental health isn't the absence of diagnosable disorders, it's better to look at it as a continuum. One side of the spectrum has the people with resilience and on the other end are the people who cause the disorders to have a severe impact on typical day to day activities. And if you have a balance, which means you are during the spectrum; you look at everything as being fine. Well, what about those days where you lack the resources for a sudden shift in change. If you are one of those people with a good balance, it's often difficult for you to recognize some of the changes that come with a sudden shift in your mental health. Here are some of the signs that you may be experiencing this sudden shift:

Changes in sleep

Different eating patterns

Isolation from friends, family and activities

Lack/loss of energy

Easily irritated

Mood swings

Performance level low at school or work

These manifestations show a decrease in emotional wellness and conceivably highlight a creating mental confusion. Probably the most widely recognized problems in youngsters and youthful grown-ups include:

Depression

Anxiety

Bipolar Disorder

Impulse Control Disorder

With disabilities, the most common are mental. disorders. Mental illnesses rank as the highest of all diseases. That's kind of a big deal for so many of us to take it lightly. According to the Health Education Authority, in any year, about 18.1% (43.6 million) of U.S. adults ages 18 years or older suffered from any mental illness and 4.2% (9.8 million) suffered from a seriously debilitating mental illness. Neuropsychiatric disorders are the leading cause of disability in the United States, accounting for 18.7% of all years of life lost to disability and premature mortality.

Suicide remains in the top 10 as the leading cause of death in the United States. Mental and physical health are interconnected. To have good physical health, your mental health has to first be healthy. For example, when you have a mental illness such as depression or anxiety, your day to day health-promoting behaviors will be affected. And vice versa, your physical health, such as chronic diseases, can have a serious impact on mental health.

Mental health is … ´the emotional and spiritual resilience which allows us to enjoy life and survive pain, disappointment and sadness. It is a positive sense of wellbeing and an underlying belief in our own, and others, dignity and worth. (Health Education Authority 1997)

When people think about physical health, it never has a negative impact on the thought process. We are either saying we need to improve in it for X, Y, and Z reason or we are happy it is a healthy lifestyle of ours. However, mental health isn't looked at in the same light. Maybe it is just now becoming a common topic in the open or maybe people are afraid to think about it. Whenever we are physically healthy, we can genuinely enjoy life to the fullest.

Just like physical health, mental health can last days, weeks, or months at a time. Physical health seems to typically be poor from simply not taking good care of ourselves. Not feeling well results in having less energy and motivation and makes it feel difficult to participate in both work and play. That is the outcome for physical and mental health. The only difference between the two is our mental health is influenced mainly by our relationships, emotions, and our ability to work.

When we feel unbalanced and our mental health is negative, we have a hard time surfing the lows of life. Versus when we have a more optimistic, stable mood because our mental wellbeing is positive, and we can cope with the ups and downs of life in a grounded, balanced way. Unlike physical health, you cannot get a mental health problem from someone else, it is not like catching a common cold or COVID-19. Either way, the effects from both can be long term. The good news is, the way we go about recovery is the same way. Physical and mental health have a codependent relationship with one another. For example, if your physical health is poor, your mental health is likely to be low as well. And on the other end of the same spectrum, if your mental health is poor, you are more likely to get ill physically.

Even though we have been taught to look at the mind and body as two different entities, mental and physical health should be looked at as the same; you cannot separate the two.

Just as poor physical health leads to poor mental health, poor mental health has a negative effect on physical health. The problem is, until recently, they have been presented as two entities, disconnected from one another. Since the founding of the NHS in 1948, there has been an increasing call on healthcare professionals to consider psychological wellbeing when treating the physical symptoms of a condition and vice versa.

How specifically does mental health affect physical health.

Over the years, we have been shown the many ways mental health has been detrimental to physical health. People who have had high levels of self-related distress over time compared to those who had the lowest rates were 32% more likely to have died from cancer. And depression has been linked to an increased risk of coronary heart disease. Then you have the associations with schizophrenia in double the risk of death from heart disease and 3x the risk of death from respiratory disease.

Makes sense that people with mental health conditions are unlikely to get the physical healthcare they need and are entitled to get. Mental health patients have been known statistically to be least likely to get even routine checks done, such as their blood pressure, weight, and cholesterol, and these help detect physical health conditions early on. This eliminates the helpful information they could use on the basic such as smoking and alcohol consumption for positive changes to their diets.

Lifestyle factors that influence the state of both your mental and physical health include exercise, diet, and smoking.

What is the link between physical and mental health?

You see the promotions for staying healthy everywhere you go, and it has become the central goal of most people's lives. It is amazing that we live in a world where there is health advice everywhere. The problem is this advice focuses on the body. Over time, researchers have investigated what influences our health and their conclusions have found that physical and mental health are even more closely related than we realized.

With health, physical health is the most common one people pay attention to.

Physical health consists of two components, nutrition and activity. There are many aspects with nutrition, the overall goal is to ensure growing bodies. For that to happen, more resources are needed about vitamins and minerals along with the appropriate amounts of protein and carbohydrates for a good balance.

Nowadays, it is more challenging as ever to make sure we all get enough exercise and physical activity, especially since COVID-19. It becomes difficult as we increase in age to change what has now developed from being habit-based to a lifestyle based. For us to be active as adults, make this a lifestyle as a child. However, no matter when you start physical fitness whether 7 or 60, making this a lifestyle will require the right MENTAL MINDSET.

Although the Department of Health and Human Services (HHS) activity guidelines recommend youth ages 6 to 17 get 60 minutes or more of physical activity each day, the majority of children get nowhere near that.

TV has always been one of the biggest distractions standing between you and a healthier lifestyle. According to the HHS, kids who watch three or more hours of TV per day are 65 percent more likely to become obese than children who watch less than one hour a day. Screen time of all types has negative effects on health, ranging from sleep loss to learning difficulty. Social media and gaming systems have increased that number drastically. While other parts of physical health require regular physical checkups, regular dental and vision checks to keep up with development and to make sure kids are getting enough sleep to fuel their growth. Discussing your concerns about your child's health as they arise can be done with the doctor during these appointments.

Be aware of the relationship physical and mental health have with one another as one entity. Here are a few ways the mind and body influence each other:

Depression directly affects the immune system, and the immune system directly affects depression.

With mental health, depression is one of the most common disorders in the United States. Depression directly affects the immune system. When the immune system has suppressed T cell responses to viruses and bacteria, this makes it more difficult to fight off anything resulting in it being easier for you to get sick and staying sick much longer. Having a weak immune system can also cause the severity of allergies or asthma.

You also have researchers seeing this vice versa where the immune system causes depression.

Stress disrupts your emotions by triggering an immune response via the brain. Inflammation from this is the driving cause of depression. To have optimal physical health, your immune system must be strong. Think of both physical and mental health when it comes to your immune system and brain. Treating one without the other only creates a vicious cycle that could become too discouraging to fix.

Mind over matter isn't always the solution with fatigue from certain mental illnesses. When you have a mood disorder such as anxiety or depression, you develop constant feelings of being tired as well as exhaustion. Proving being mentally tired leads to physical tiredness. Chronically depressed and anxious people lack of energy keeps them least likely to make a habit of exercising and are more likely to quit early when they do. The persistent tiredness also interferes with basic hygiene.

Outbursts from anger and stress from anxiety badly affect the heart.

An Australian study has proven that acute emotions can cause heart attacks. Dr. Thomas Buckley, lead author of the study, said,

"Our findings confirm what has been suggested in prior studies and anecdotal evidence…that episodes of intense anger can act as a trigger for a heart attack." The studies concluded following an episode of intense anger puts a person at risk for a heart attack 8.5 times higher than average. This number increases with anxiety, putting it at a 9.5-fold. Now that we understand the relationship between mental health and physical health, how do I try to improve my mental health. Although mental health has become more of an open topic to where the shame has been lifted from most, there are still people who feel embarrassed discussing it. Whether you feel ashamed to openly discuss the topic or you don't and still want to do what you can from the privacy of your own personal space. Here are some steps you can take on your own to improve your Mental Health:

Self-Care is the best start to have improvements in Mental Health. Self-care involves taking action within your control for the optimal intention being to improve your current mental state.

Learn what boundaries are and then implement them within your life. Then become self-aware so you can cope with the ups and downs of life. Here are a few tips to start with:

Implement a sleep schedule.

When you don't get enough sleep, you increase the chances of mental health problems.

According to Harvard Medical School, individuals with a history of insomnia are four times as likely to develop depression. Conversely, over 50 percent of people with anxiety and up to 90 percent of people with depression experience sleep problems of some kind.

Sleep is especially sensitive with children. With already weak immune systems, children can suffer from even lower immune systems if they do not receive enough. With a higher chance of having problems in academic performance, behavior, and decreased mental health overall. Setting a sleep schedule can be as simple as limiting activities that interrupt your sleep cycle, scheduling a sleep routine. If you need help relaxing before going to sleep, you should do things such as: relax an hour before bedtime, drink a warm glass of milk, drink your favorite herbal tea blend, or meditate.

There's a reason the doctor says to go outside more for your Vitamin D. Getting outside in nature does a body good. Nowadays, children, adolescents, and especially adults fail to get enough time outside. Your body has a natural need to want to be outside, so when you lack the motivation to go outside, this is your body's way of letting you know there is a problem. Depression has decreased your motivation to want to get outside. As discussed before, this must be the ego working against you because getting outside to walk in nature has been known to reduce your symptoms of depression. Getting outside the house for just 20 minutes makes a huge difference in your mood while improving your mental health.

Schedule times to do activities in your planner.

Writing things down help with your commitment to bring things into physical form. It has been proven that participating in activities that involve your hands reduce symptoms of depression and improve overall mental health. It is always a good time to take a class or take up a new hobby for the sake of your mental health.

If all else fails, seeking treatment is the most appropriate step to take. Self-care is very important with your mental health. Making self-care a lifestyle change keeps you with a healthy, consistent mental frame of mind. Sometimes things happen in life that turn things so upside down for us we have to seek outside help for the appropriate treatments. And that is okay.

Now we understand the importance of having both physical and mental healthy lifestyles for healthy balance. To give the best of you from within stay fit and lit.

"Good habits are hard to form and easy to live with. Bad habits are easy to form and hard to live with. Pay attention. Be aware. If we don't consciously form good ones, we will unconsciously form bad ones." -Morgan Musk

CHAPTER 4

Self-love or Selfish

Monologue:

I am a woman hear me.

I'm so powerful as a woman that it takes more than one thing to define me. I wear a magnitude of different hats.

Want to know the main thing that makes me more powerful than a man?

I give life, men can't do that.

I have such a big heart; it allows me to show unconditional love to my child and enemies within the same flow.

I live within my own rules with a natural need to grow.

I uplift the next woman as much as possible.

As a Queen, I know how hard things can get living in a "man's world."

I allow men to treat me like the Queen I am and allow the man to be my King if the crown fits.

My crown stays perfectly fitted at all times due to the strength of my core I know balance.

My superpower is me being a woman, now watch me roar.

Every Prince needs his Queen.

My child saved my life, because of him, I was forced to figure out how to love myself unconditionally so I can be able to love him the same if not more. If you do not love yourself, you will never be able to love others.

Early in my life, I would put so much time and effort into others at the expense of myself. I would feel guilty if I bought myself something I wanted, knowing that someone I cared about needed the very same thing. I kept other people satisfied and would not always feel like I got the same treatment in return, this eventually made me feel worthless. I was giving for the wrong reasons. Although I would treat other people how I wanted them to treat me, they didn't, which eventually led to me being a people pleaser and that depleted me completely. I felt invisible and like no one cared, which led to despair. I thought doing things for myself was a selfish act, I don't know where I got this from because it was totally not true. Knowledge has been my power. Love can brighten up anyone's soul.

Ego - "I" personality - and symbol 'self-made in the mind to secure self-appreciation/overly confidence. Delicate to self-evaluation and being misunderstood. Attracted to naming both self as well as other people.

I know my ego can be selfish, but my inner child needs self-love.

Choosing yourself isn't considered selfish. It is actually the first step in self-love.

To obtain self-love, you have to spend time with yourself doing the things you love starting with a new hobby, doing things for self-care, or rewarding yourself with a trip.

I dated myself for a while, doing many things I always wanted to do and even though at first, it felt uncomfortable, it ended up being absolutely amazing.

Figure out the things that bring you joy by living through your inner child.

Sometimes it takes seeing life through the eyes of a child to really explore. What are some things you liked doing as a child? I think it is fair to say I loved a little bit of everything. From writing scripts to playing basketball to teaching, dancing, you name it, I had fun with it all. How did I get so wrapped up into these activities, to begin with? I didn't give it too much thought, I reckon, I figured it would be fun, so I tried it and focused only on having fun with it. Every hobby I had and enjoyed as a child, I enjoy even more as an adult.

As a child, we would have a dream one minute and leave it to our imaginations the next to run wild with it. We created these illusions in our mind then brought them to life. And it was so much fun. What happened to the inner child within? It is called Adulting, but why does adulting have to have a serious connotation behind it? Why can't we live through our inner child as much as possible but still be responsible? Somewhere between sleepovers in a tent and paying bills, we took life way too seriously. Not necessarily because we have to, the more so because we feel that is how you respond to life situations. What if we took the emotions out of the equation, stop overthinking it, or talk ourselves out of being happy. Children never need a reason to explore and have fun, they just do. They enjoy the small things in life we now take for granted as adults. I rediscovered my inner child once I had my son. I would watch him have the most fun exploring from room to room. He would get tunnel vision when he came across the perfect item that typically stood out or looked breakable.

Making sure your needs are always met first is selfishness. Making sure your needs are not always met last is self-love.

What is the difference between selfishness and self-love?

Is there truly a way to tend to yourself without being selfish? What does it look like to have self-love? Feeling bad after saying no to someone you care about. Saying yes to things you really do not want to do. Do you worry more about the well-being and needs of others over yourself? Often running yourself into exhaustion just to make sure you are showing up for others. Then you definitely have a fear of selfishness and it is blocking your expression of self-love. When a person has boundaries, feels comfortable saying no, and can put their personal needs and dreams first even when someone may need something different from you at the time, this person has self-love. Some people still look at these actions as selfishness. They know mentally that it is self-love, but at the core still feel bad. Not knowing the difference between selfishness and self-love can cause anxiety, exhaustion and unhappiness. There are many people who suffer from "fear of selfishness" syndrome. We have all heard the importance behind the ideas of many teachings that to love someone else, you must first love yourself.

In some teachings, the word for compassion is simultaneously for both self and others because the two cannot be separated. Same as with love, to feel compassion for someone else, you must first feel it for yourself. And somehow people still struggle with practicing self-love.

Bottled down by the fear of being selfish, many people do whatever it takes to be there for other people. We do this even when it causes us to slow down on our goals and drains us of our energy.

When this happens, you will know it from feeling as if you have worn yourself thin. You have feelings of resentment due to the overwhelming and overloading feeling you have. Once a person has drained themself to exhaustion, you carry around guilt and ultimately lose the ability to show up for others in an authentic way.

How do you protect yourself and others from resentment, upset, or guilt that naturally arises from overextending yourself? Boundaries! Seriously, boundaries changed everything for me. Just like fences/gates around a house in place to protect your space from the other person's personal space, boundaries do the same for people. Boundaries are your way of letting people know how to treat you. You either have loose boundaries almost to nonexistent, meaning anything goes with you, you have no rules for your life, and you expect others to not have them as well. When the other person you are connecting with has boundaries and you don't, you will constantly feel offended with theirs in place because yours isn't.

When both people have boundaries, it is easier to communicate.

Growing up in an enmeshed family, you never have boundaries, and although you are unfamiliar with what they are, you recognize them as something others do have. Setting boundaries as an adult felt weird for me when I started to have some, and I constantly felt guilt when I had to put them in place. I'm happy I discovered them because now I feel safe and protected without the unnecessary distress from tedious situations that does not have anything to do with what happens behind your fences. You see the other person's problems in their yard, you recognize them, and may have empathy for it, but that is as far as it goes for you. Now that you know when to be self-attentive and when to be generous, you've created something so powerful that gives you healthier relationships and better peace of mind.

Okay, that may sound simpler said than done and the question remains, how can you recognize "fear of selfishness"? Selfishness comes in the form of shame. You feel some type of way after saying no and sometimes pissed that you said yes, never feeling as if you had a choice in the matter. Leaving you with feelings of feeling overloaded, resentful, and burnt-out.

When you are being authentic and give from the heart, you feel great. This leaves for connection and openness towards the person you are giving to. When you give out of the wrong reasons, you are left with a feeling of being drained and tense. When you want to run, escape, or hide far off in the middle of nowhere, this is because you are having fears of selfishness. This may drive you to give, but when you do, it is measured doses and with less enthusiasm.

In contrast, self-love gives us feelings of openness, empathy, and eagerness to make a difference whenever you can. This gives us the ease to feel joy. Once you show up as your best self, you are able to be a part of win-win situations. After all, what facts points to you being selfish? More than likely, if you are reading this, then you're probably not selfish. Selfish people wouldn't be concerned about the balance of things, to begin with. Being curious about how to not be selfish eliminates the chances of you being that way.

"The greatest gift you can give to somebody is your own personal development. I used to say, "If you will take care of me, I will take care of you." Now I say, "I will take care of me for you if you will take care of you for me."

— Jim Rohn

Such a beautiful way of saying it.

You may be wondering when does self-love become selfish?

Unconditional love is merciful, forgiving, and kind. When you love yourself fully you can love the differences in others.

When stuck in self-pity, making everything about yourself, then it is easy for selfishness to ease in. The trick is to take the attention from yourself and put it back onto others or else the slope is slippery down to selfishness. Other people's opinions of you are none of your business and pay attention to the fact that it is an opinion and not a fact. Facts over feelings.

Knowing you are in a good place helps you get others there as well and is a big part of self-love.

In staying focused on the facts, I don't see how self-love can ever be selfish, considering you can never love others, if you do not love yourself. Having self-awareness is the key to it all. Because how you treat others is really how you view yourself.

The interplay between self-love and selfishness comes down to this.

- When we are adequately loving on ourselves, the insecurities we have about ourselves becomes smaller with more focus being on a way to be there for other people.
- You cannot pour from an empty cup; therefore, when focusing on refilling ourselves with self-care, we need to keep open communication with people we are the closest to.
- It is a win-win situation when we have less judgment due to more love. This love radiates into better treatment of ourselves and reflected into how we treat others.

Time to shift from a scarcity mindset with fear of selfishness to an abundance mindset full of love for yourself.

"A million likes will not make you like yourself." – Nicole Floss

You don't have to present selfies to show that you love yourself. Indeed, you don't have to inform anybody concerning that. Notwithstanding, your activities and contemplations ought to mirror the affection you feel towards yourself. To assist you with beginning, here are three different ways you can rehearse self-esteem:

Be mindful of how you converse with yourself.

It's anything but difficult to lose control of the little inward pundit that sits inside you. The most ideal approach to dodge this from happening is to get mindful of it. Try not to battle it or blow up with it. Rather, converse with it with affection and benevolence. Ask yourself, "Is this something I would state to my closest companion?" And, "How might I put a more certain and strong turn on this?" The more you practice this, the simpler it becomes.

Be kind towards your body.

Converse with it and treat it as though it was somebody you love. Try not to utilize practice as a discipline yet as something that gets the positive endorphins moving. Discover a movement you appreciate doing and anticipate doing, as opposed to something you fear. Converse with your body decidedly, as well, and routinely offer thanks to your preferred parts. It probably won't be great, and there may be pieces you'd prefer to improve, yet it is a brilliant sanctuary keeping you alive here on planet Earth.

Learn to get praises with elegance.

On the off chance that somebody praises you, grin and state much obliged. This may sound senseless and maybe you as of now do this, yet there is a shockingly high number of individuals who battle with this. I used to be one of those individuals as well. Luckily, today, I acknowledge them, I appreciate them, and I trust them. You ought to as well. Something that can help with this is to likewise improve at offering out commendations. It's fun and satisfying and gets positive energy into each connection.

CHAPTER 5

There is always a Choice (Power of Faith)

"The Pursuit of happiness is a matter of choice." – Charles R. Swindoll

Just like Faith is a Choice.

We all have a choice between Fear or Faith. They cannot coexist.

F-E-A-R Has two meanings:

Forget Everything and Run.

OR

Face Everything and Rise. The choices is yours.

Everything is a Choice.

Everything in life is a choice. I understand there are some events in life we cannot change. The power lies in how you CHOOSE to react to these events. We are not always going to make the right choices in life and sometimes we may have to choose among what seems to be nothing but bad options. Regardless of the situation, it is always your choice.

"Everything in your life is a reflection of a choice you have made. If you want a different result, make a difference choice"

- Stormi McKnight

Unless a conscious choice to change has been made, no change will happen. As previously discussed, there are ways to handle the actions of others. Being proactive in your response instead of reactive, we eliminate the stress and anger. You cannot change another human being no matter how hard we try. When we choose to focus on ourselves, we realize that we can only change ourselves. The only thing we can change about another individual, is their view of the world. That is so exciting about being a life coach. People come to me only when they want to change something about their lives. Even though the client is doing the hard work, I get a chance to help you look at the choices you've made in life and challenge you to decide if you want to make the choice for change. Ultimately you are the only one who makes the choices to do so.

Feeling as if we have options makes a huge difference to our state of mind and seeing the situation as under control, gives us the power we need. When these decisions are being made, they may bring some strong unwanted emotions such as fear. This is a normal feeling and all a part of the growth process. Simply readjusting your mistakes is part of feeling empowered. If you are not familiar with choices or need to relearn, start off small. Start by making choices like choosing an outfit to wear or what you should eat, similar to the way a toddler might do it.

When you understand that we always have a choice, it also becomes a constant reminder of the power we truly have within. We have the power to be our authentic self and to take control of the life you have. The scary part about this is looking at the choices we have already made that led us to the life we have. You can see it as something frightening or something liberating.

Let's start living a life of conscious choices. What choices will you make in your life today?

Generational Curses.

Sometimes the choices we make are not our own. Have you ever thought about what influences the decisions made in your life? Or are you sure you know what drives them?

Human beings have a complex operating system, yet we are subjected to the same simple ways of making choices as that of pets with the most simplistic operating systems, such as a cat. For example, with a pet cat trying to decide whether to jump on the sofa, his choice is easily influenced by the events surrounding him and the actions of others. Even though we are subjected to the same behavior as human beings, ours are more subtle.

For example, in a recent study at Ohio State University, there were surveys done for campus sexual behavior. They found that over time women have consistently lied about the number of sexual partners they have had compared to men. What sparked the attention of the people conducting the survey is that the numbers looked fishy from women compared to that of men. Only once the women thought they were doing the survey hooked to a lie detector test they revealed the truth. Then the discrepancy between the male and female reposting vanished, because the women's numbers rose. Even though the survey was anonymous, and the data was being collected for useful scientific purposes, still with that moment of decision making the women allowed for something to mentally persuade them to round down their numbers. This is called stereotype threat.

Human beings behave in a way they think they are expected to behave.

This is in subtle, consistent ways.

The effects of this study showed up in a lot of things. The stereotype threat was used with races as well:

When reminding Black students that Black people are assumed to be dumb, they did consistently worse on tests. When a reminder to Asian students they are known to be academically good with math, they did better in math. The study showed how you can make black or white people better or worse at golf just by using fear of either stereotype. Facts over feelings. There is data on this. The conclusion being that people's decisions can be easily changed by small assumptions and stimuli.

The question now is where do these ideas come from? The answer was narrowed down to microaggressions. Microaggressions can be the different ways one's identity, and a person's status is reflected back throughout a day. This is all the ways we feel less than, reminders of who people want us to be, and different ways people try to put us in our place. Society tries to make men feel as if they are only valued from their success and money, picking at their masculinity but constantly making you feel the need to be in competition with other men. As if you have to always win. Society views women differently based on insinuations you are not attractive solely on the standard of what that is. Making women feel as if their value lies in their looks, or that we are not whole. Little by little, these microaggressions can be dealt with, but what about when they add up over time. This eventually draws attention to the microinequities. The unfair things in life and constant reminders of how certain people get the short end of the stick no matter what. This causes prejudices to make other decisions for them.

These microinequities arise from the decisions people make based on prejudices they don't know they have. Society tells us how we should feel about others based on the things displayed on TV, stories that make it to the news, articles, and comments said among acquaintances and friends. They will never outright say they don't like a certain race based on deep-seated prejudices. They will say they have no problem with a person based on their skin color, but when the time comes to make an ethical decision, it often gets tipped in the wrong direction. We have no control over the factors that got us to this point in life. These stereotypes were taught since we came from the cradle. There is too much pressure in trying to control what others expect of us. We can try to actively unlearn bad habits and wrong experiences, but we are all fallible.

We forgive ourselves by realizing that our choices are not made in a vacuum, which means they will never be fully our choices. Believe it or not, we tell the lies we have been trained to tell. We make mistakes wholly on expectations. It is a slippery slope, but we often fall prey to the patterns built within. Although nothing can free us from a lifetime of these patterns being trained within, self-awareness helps us to recognize them more and more. By recognizing these things, we fall into them less and less.

I've had people to be obnoxious towards me, after realizing that the choices to be that way isn't their own, this made it easier to forgive them. Regardless of the situation, people still need to be held accountable for their actions. Although it is never easy to break toxic patterns, people need to be encouraged to work against their worst impulses. Showing mercy to yourself allows for you to show mercy towards others. Most of the time, people have belief systems that keep them trapped in doing only what others expect them to do. When you judge someone so harshly instead of showing compassion, consider the fact that maybe you are only doing so because of how you too were raised.

Everyone has a right to make choices. What if your choices were taken away? Choices such as: where to work, live, who to spend time with, what you can buy and spend money on? Older adults and the disabled often are put in situations where someone else has the power to decide for them. People often need supported decision making to make decisions of their own, have control over their lives, with the necessary help to do so.

How is it that we make choices? Supported Decision-Making is a unique way of describing who we all make our choices. There isn't a day that goes by that we do not need help making a decision. In situations with the lack of understanding to properly file your taxes, whether to pay for certain repairs with your car, or a diagnosis that sounds like a foreign language. How do you typically deal with these situations? More than likely, we ask people the closest to us, such as a friend or a family member or someone they know who can speak more of our language in explaining things. It is common sense to seek help when you do not know enough to make a good decision. Going to people experienced or educated in these matters is when you are using Supported Decision-Making. Getting this help leads you to make a better decision.

Older adults and people with disabilities make decisions the same way. They have the same rights as everyone else. They can work, live, and love like everyone else, which gives them the right to use supported decision making like everyone else. It is normal to run across people who may need more help than average or helped in different ways than usual.

CHAPTER 6

Alone, not Lonely (Freedom and Independence)

Committing to traveling alone made me feel like a superwoman, actually doing it gave me my superwoman powers.

Voyaging alone will be the most startling, most freeing, groundbreaking experience of your life. Attempt it at any rate once.

If you're waiting for someone to travel with you...you may wait a lifetime.

Bitterness is what I felt sitting there thinking about how I cancelled my trip to Paris because the guy I was with at the time was making another excuse not to go to Paris with me, and after half of my friends backed out of this trip, it felt like I would never get to go. What if they back out the next time as well when I'm ready and prepared to go? Does that mean I never get to go? So many negative thoughts entered my mind about something that seemed so simple. As I picked up my bucket list to see what I can do on my own besides traveling, I saw that on my bucket list to go on a trip solo. I grew excited and scared at the same time. Excited at the possibility I can still go on my trip, scared thinking about going by myself. Immediately I committed to a decision to go because I knew I was not the only one who ever thought about pursuing this. Immediately

I researched safe places, safe places for women, and every piece of information I needed to make this happen. After reading several articles and looking at tons of pictures, I started to get back excited.

Ladies need genuine snapshots of isolation and self-reflection to adjust the amount of ourselves we part with.

There are tools, resources, and apps for going anywhere you want and getting anything, you need. There are beautiful moments in taking risk on your own. There are complications and fear in many things you do by yourself, that is the very reason you should do it.

To be strong, learn to go at it alone. Whenever I would plan a trip, it was always with others my entire life, I wasn't even aware that people went on trips by themselves. As most people know, for planning a trip with others, you run into frustrations due to people backing out at the last minute or different preferences or certain things some want to do over others and have to compromise on so many things you shouldn't have to compromise on when you pay your money. There were so many trips I had to drop because of everyone backing out and I get that life happens unexpectantly, but where does that continue to leave me?

It wasn't until a girlfriend had just come back from traveling internationally and was telling me about everything she did and experienced with such vibrant energy, I had to ask who all she went with because it seemed like everything went really smooth on her trip. Her response was she went by herself. I had even more questions about it because this was unheard of where I'm from. Foreign language. She looked puzzled that I've never thought of doing it myself as much as I like to travel. Well, after that conversation, I did research on women traveling alone and so many things pulled up.

Blogs about personal experience, articles about safest countries for women to visit solo, reasons women love traveling solo. I had discovered a new world and was ready to go somewhere immediately.

Growing up, I learned how to be independent at a young age, so going into my adult years it always came naturally for me. It felt great to have what I saw as the equivalent to control over my life. Responsibility embeds empowerment. Independence at the time was me not depending on others and the feeling of being free from outside control. Having this, I didn't understand why I didn't feel as free. Did independence equal freedom? Although I had control over my life, I didn't feel as if I had as much power. By gaining independence early on, I developed certain structures in my life that worked for me at the time. In my realization that if I wanted to be free, I needed to be comfortable with being uncomfortable to change without constraint. Some people look at freedom and independence as the same thing, although they both are intuitive words that most see as something familiar to understand. They actually differ in its meaning when it comes to the context. I desperately needed to feel free after breaking away from what others tried to lead as controlling lives, which led me to finally tackle some things off of my bucket list. I realized that by experiencing the things I've always wanted to do before I die gives me the feeling of being free.

Some things left on my Bucket List at the time.

- Skydiving
- Traveling internationally solo
- Spend a month traveling with only 6 outfits

- Reconnect with past close friends and take an International trip with one.
- Go on a road trip.
- Take an improv class
- Ride on an elephant
- Meditation Retreat
- Ride a horse on the beach
- Start some hobbies
- Date myself for a few months
- Abs
- Tattoo
- Hip hop class

I've completed them all except two. And yes, I celebrated myself after doing so.

My independence gave me the choice to do skydiving and in doing so, I felt free. It gave me the ability to let everything else go and just live in that moment.

Independence is absolute because you do not depend on anyone and freedom is subjective to location and time. Both come with trust and responsibilities. And independence leads to freedom. For example, after the Civil War, slaves were considered "freed." The confusion is in the language. Discriminatory laws were still in existence and Black Americans were not allowed to do as they pleased. Which means they had independence, not freedom. It wasn't until equal treatment was given to everyone that they were truly free in the sense of the word.

Although independence can lead to freedom, it is not a prerequisite for freedom. A child can be dependent upon their parents and still feel freedom. Freedom is a state of mind, you are free when you feel free.

"If you want to be strong, learn to fight alone." – Shubham Singh Dhanda

Life became exhausting with so many challenges to face on my own. I knew I was drained. Here I am thousands of miles away from any support (or lack thereof) as a newly single mom working two Full-Time jobs, taking a Self-Help Class, still working physically and mentally in my daily regimen, and getting an average of 4 hours of sleep a day. I was on the verge of a nervous breakdown and wanted to feel free from it all.

Traveling alone was an impulse decision and the best one I've made. When becoming comfortable with being uncomfortable by stepping outside of your comfort zone, this gives influence on the person you are when you step back in. With only 6 outfits in my luggage and a last-minute plan to spontaneously travel to places my fingers touched on the globe (the two out of three that made my bucket list at least). I remember the feeling of excitement to immerse myself in a world of the unknown throughout Southeast Asia. I've never been to this part of the world and this was my first solo trip internationally. I got frustrated with waiting for others to travel with me and, over time, researched the experiences of other women doing the same thing. I know in life there will be highs and lows and it is important to be balanced in dealing with both aspects. I was having a hard time surfing the lows. This was shortly after my Postpartum depression. My Post Traumatic Stress Disorder was triggered, so I was on leave from my primary job due to circumstances beyond my control and I had just quit the second full-time job a couple of months previously. As a newly single mom to an almost 2-year-old I had so many questions about the silent battles I faced. I remember the desperation to feel free of it all. Earlier on, I made a promise to myself to become comfortable with being uncomfortable. So, it was a no brainer. This was the perfect time to do this, so I did, good thing I got this out of my system shortly before COVID-19 happened. Traveling solo gives you the self-confidence you need to tap into your natural superwoman powers. For a person who struggled with the learned behavior of codependent issues to a superwoman who travels internationally solo.

'Being alone for a while is dangerous. It's addicting. Once you see how peaceful it is, you don't want to deal with people anymore' - Tom Hardy

It wasn't until I forced myself to be alone that I realized I had issues with being alone. Over time, I sought the help to discover why. This was largely in part due to my abandonment issues as a child and me watching my mom break down every time my father left as if she couldn't make it on her own.

When a person travels alone this is an act of confidence. Doing this by yourself shows strength. This is a correlation between self-esteem and traveling. As licensed psychologist Dr. Chloe Carmichael Peet stated, "If you do something that requires a certain amount of strength or independence, you then see yourself as a stronger and more independent person. Your behavior is reinforcing a positive self-esteem. As your self-esteem grows, you start engaging in more independent, self-serving behaviors." In doing my research of women traveling solo, I remember the feelings I would get from all the positive expressions in the pictures they took. As we strive more and more to be women who take charge, we become the woman we always wanted to be. Which is a woman who is decisive enough to pick up and go whenever she wants and having the confidence in while doing so.

Where does the power to be alone come from?

Although I've always loved adventures, previously, I did not see myself as the type of person who could decide to do something that requires so much courage. Whenever I was on IG, usually I saw rich girls taking exotic solo travels and seemed as if they had no care in the world. My situation was different. Besides, I would usually look to my excuses to justify not going by myself. I remember thinking about things such as the risk of traveling alone, no accountability partner, having to take on the role of so many things with no error left to chance. Working my way through so many things people are usually fearful of. You have people who feel uncomfortable being alone in the privacy of their own home and even more so in the public. Alone with private judgments of ourselves and in public with the fear of judgment from others. Once you reach the point of not needing constant stimulation and company, you feel extremely empowered and have finally reached the ability to be okay with being by yourself.

It is always rewarding to feel the fear and do it anyway. When doing things solo, such as traveling, it increases your choices and eliminates being contingent upon what others want. You are thinking about what makes you happy and what you want to experience.

You're still out in the world with others but have the time to yourself to reflect and regroup.

After experiencing the first solo destination, things became easier. Overall, because of these experiences, my confidence has increased, self-esteem healthier, and my decision-making opened up positive changes in my everyday life. All of this from an empowering and enjoyable experience. Traveling anywhere gives you the same benefits whether going to far destinations or the ones close by. I experienced traveling alone to close by places before I jumped internationally. And with both, I have different personal learning experiences. Being in complete control every step of the way took away the anxiety and lack of self-worth I had before the experience. Remember to start small, remember why you are there, and know it will get easier.

Here is a list of things that solo traveling teaches you:

1. You will not die of embarrassment.
2. How to Be Lonely
3. How to make friends
4. What you want to be when you grow up.
5. The world is mostly good.
6. Independence
7. Confidence
8. Experience the taste of freedom.
9. Better at being alone and managing feelings of loneliness.
10. Increases your research and planning abilities.

CHAPTER 7

Redefining Your Self-Worth

"Maturity is learning to walk away from people and situations that threaten your peace of mind, self-respect, values, morals or self-worth." – Sudarshan Jha

What are selfies doing to self-esteem?

Triggers insecurity, anxiety, and depression.

A poll was taken in 2015 with the curiosity of how much time girls spend taking selfies and found that for ages 16 – 25 the average is 5+ hours a week. Taking selfies can be a tedious process. Women average 10 – 20 shots to get one image. With so many apps nowadays, the filtering and editing process can take some time, considering you now have apps that can erase pimples, change your bone structure, and slim your waistline. The possibilities are endless. Selfies can easily go from being silly to resulting in you measuring yourself worth. As if it wasn't enough, we had to see airbrushed models in magazines, nowadays, young people get to use the same images editing software to be the models themselves. Think about it, you have to constantly self-analyze yourself to fix every single thing you see as a flaw trying to perfect it. Which leads you to comparisons of other people's photos.

Seeking perfection.

Ever since we've gotten the option to take our pictures that use to be final and have post-production, it sends a different message other than you are beautiful just the way that you are. You do have some filters that distort your image in a fun, amusing way, and also the ones called the "pretty filter" on Instagram and Snapchat. Trying to create flawless pictures has become a habit that has *increased* so drastically that it is second nature to airbrush and instantly feel some type of way about yourself based on what appears to be flawless pictures on your daily online. With so many possibilities of photo editing while living in a society that values appearances it gets easier to be scrutinized by others while doing the same to peers.

The comparison traps.

Social media has been set up to compare yourself to other people. When engaging with social media in this way daily, your self-esteem is bound to take a hit. In one study, it was proven that by constantly strolling, looking at selfies decreases a satisfying life, and your self-esteem plummets. In another study, it was concluded that girls who spent more time looking at their pictures on social media became critical of their weight and objectified themselves. Before social media, adults grew up with that much needed alone time in their head, nowadays that has been eroded. All free time has now been dedicated to constantly checking different forms of social media. Then falling prey to comparison. The way you see yourself on the outside has to match how you feel on the outside or else even if you receive a million likes, you still have insecurities. Humans have mood consistencies. For instance, when feeling low, you may be more likely to listen to something sad instead of some type of mood enhancer like a comedy. Whenever you are feeling negatively towards yourself, remember that taking a good selfie is not a good solution.

Mental health consequences

Even though social media isn't the cause of mental health disorders, it can trigger people already struggling with depression and anxiety. Comparisons lead to you devaluing yourself more. Due to the increase in people fixating more on their appearance due to social media, people are developing a term closely related to body dysmorphic disorder called selfie dysmorphia. Body dysmorphic disorder is a mental health disorder closely related to OCD. Meaning people with this are obsessive over what they perceive to be body image flaws. Some are imagined, some overexaggerated, and others as simple as a blemish. Regardless of how minor these flaws, maybe they are all equally blown out of proportion.

Even if some never reach the so-called selfie dysmorphia, they are still on the spectrum somewhere still fixated on their appearance.

- Being more mindful about social media.
- Building self-esteem
- Depression
- Anxiety
- Obsessive Perfectionism
- Cognitive Distortions
- Abuse

How do we develop a healthy counterbalance to social media pressures? A good place to start is to evaluate the ways you are navigating your social media. Limiting your conversations about the photos you post and see. Lead by example and make sure you are conscious of the number of pictures you are asking your children to take. A photo every now and then is fine and allows you to prioritize actually being in the moment. When you take your child to any event, don't allow them to experience it all through the lens of a camera. Instead, show them that by simply being there, that within itself is good enough. Parents should set an example for phone etiquette as well. Processing your emotional state and reasons you are picking up your phone. Would you so happen to be anxious? If so, why? Maybe you are anxious because of picking up your phone to constantly check social media.

Having a plan can help with being mindful. Such as monitoring how long you stay on, giving yourself a time limit. What are you getting on there for, are you checking something in particular or merely getting on from habit? And most importantly, be prepared to observe how being on there makes you feel. If it is making you feel bad about yourself, then be prepared to put it down. In a society that constantly seeks external validation through different social media, has led to an increase of people prioritizing their appearance. Selfies hold a stigma saying that how I look is more important than anything. Instead, we should be sending the message that what women think and do is even more important. I know we have a habit of complimenting appearances, but we should redirect our focus on the things people do and how hard they work. It is important to have many sources of self-esteem. For long term happiness, you have to feed your inner core by doing the things you care about.

Skills grow by putting time and effort into a personal interest. Seeing this is what makes you proud of what you can do. This eliminates trying to achieve perfection by seeing that is certainly impossible. These redirects girls focus from external validation in compliments to looking within for self-esteem. This is the only way you're capable of consistent growth into a genuinely happy and confident woman.

The importance of self-esteem and its dimensions.

Self-esteem reflects what your worth and value is based upon your beliefs. It deprives from your sense of worthiness or unworthiness based on the feelings people experience. Your self-esteem has a huge impact on the choices and decisions we make. A person with a healthy self-esteem takes care of themselves and work towards their full potential. People with high self-esteem consistently work to fulfill their personal goals. People with low self-esteem don't see themselves as being worthy of happy outcomes or the ability to therefore procrastinate with important things becoming less persistent, resilient, lacking the ability to overcome adversity. Although the goals of people with high self-esteem versus the ones with low may be the same, the difference lies in the motivation to pursue them.

Self-esteem can be looked at as abstract because it is difficult for someone who do not possess it to know what it is like to have it. A person who takes good care of themselves believes in their importance and value. Making good decisions improves your value.

Be as picky with your men as you are with your selfies.

There are dimensions to self-esteem.

High vs Low: This is determined by your thoughts and feelings about your worth. Proportionality of Self-Esteem: Some people have high self-esteem due to a series of accomplishments. They celebrate themselves for overcoming real challenges in life. You have people who have high self-esteem that are unaligned with actual accomplishments and actions. Their high self-esteem is based on the high self-opinion they have of themselves. These are the people who walk around with a sense of entitlement. This way of thinking is not healthy and can be looked at as "overly-inflated" narcissism.

This doesn't mean people with low self-esteem have not met adversity, challenges, or treated others well. They generally feel good about themselves. Then you have the people who have a healthy self-esteem but have mental issues that make it hard to recognize accomplishments and actions as meaningful. They include:

Continuing to hold themselves to a higher standard internally causes emotional distress and the display of low self-esteem. However, someone on the outside looking into the situation see them as worthy based upon their accomplishments and actions. Because of this, the outside observer has difficulty understanding their reason for feeling bad about themselves.

Self -esteem is a complex topic and cannot be simplified away with high vs low dimensions alone. It varies based upon being reasonable, the magnitude, and comparisons of accomplishments and actions. To develop a balanced healthy self-esteem, both dimensions should be nurtured and cultivated.

With connection being a natural part of our human species, low self-esteem is often challenged in our interactions. This can be from people starting a new school or job to people forming new friendships and relationships. Having a healthy self-esteem ensures characteristics such as

- Acting independent and mature
- Taking pride in accomplishments and achievements
- Accepting frustration then dealing with it responsibly
- Trying new things and challenges
- Helping others when possible

People with low self-esteem avoid situations with possible failure, fear of embarrassment, and are judged for mistakes. Low self-esteem can lead to issues such as:

- Trouble in relationships
- Difficult time making friends
- Experiencing negative moods from shame and sadness to anxiety and anger.
- Low motivation
- Poor body image
- Sexual activity at a young age.
- Self-medicating to feel better.

Causes of low self-esteem

- Parents who are unsupportive
- Toxic friendships
- Stressful life events

- Abuse or trauma
- Performing poorly at school
- Setting unrealistic goals
- Depression
- Anxiety
- Bullying
- Loneliness
- Constant medical issues

Signs of low self-esteem

- Avoidance with new things
- Turning down opportunities
- Feeling unwanted/unloved
- Playing a victim role by blaming others for your own mistakes.
- Unable to deal with frustration
- Negative self-talk
- Comparisons
- Fearing failure or embarrassment
- Challenges with making friends
- Low motivation
- Inability to take compliments

- Easily distressed

Self-worth is defined by Merriam-Webster as:

"a feeling that you are a good person who deserves to be treated with respect."

Self-worth vs Self-esteem

Nowadays self-worth has been used interchangeably with self-esteem. Except self-worth is more so about valuing your worth as a person from the core and less about measuring yourself based on external actions. Self-worth = who you are and self-esteem = what you do.

Society has focused on having a high self-esteem which seems healthy. The issue is the focus is measuring ourselves against others instead of attention to core values. We keep hearing from our competitive culture that to feel good about ourselves we have to be above average to feel special. Problem is we cannot all be above average. You set yourself up for a losing battle when you search for self-worth by constantly comparing ourselves to others. As Dr. Neff says, "There is always someone richer, more attractive, or more successful than we are.

Self-Worth vs. Self-Esteem

Although, self-worth is often used as a synonym for "self-esteem," Dr. Lisa Firestone believes that self-worth should be less about measuring yourself based on external actions and more about valuing your inherent worth as a person. Self-worth is about who you are, not about what you do. And even when we manage to feel self-esteem for one golden moment, we can't hold on to it. Our sense of self-worth bounces around like a ping-pong ball, rising and falling in lockstep with our latest success or failure."

Your mental health becomes damaged when you are constantly seeking external validation for your self-worth.

One study at the University of Michigan found that college students who base their self-worth on external sources (including academic performance, appearance and approval from others) reported more stress, anger, academic problems and relationship conflicts. They also had higher levels of alcohol and drug use, as well as more symptoms of eating disorders. The same study found that students who based their self-worth on internal sources, not only felt better, they also received higher grades and were less likely to use drugs and alcohol or to develop eating disorders.

As you build your sense of self, accomplishments are important to acknowledge. However, the focus should be on what makes you are important for the unique qualities you consider for your self-worth. As mindfulness expert Dr. Donna Rockwell points out, we are all unique and that gives each of us inherent value. According to Dr. Firestone, "We shouldn't be rating ourselves, we should just be ourselves."

Building Self-Worth

To move forward with increasing your self-worth, you must first stop comparing yourself with others and evaluating your every move. You can do this by challenging your critical inner voice. These constant destructive thought patterns are like nasty coaches in our heads with an internal dialogue undermining our sense of self-worth leading to destructive maladaptive behaviors.

The importance of self-worth and how we can increase ours?

There is a reason certain words start with self. We have self-esteem, self-compassion, self-acceptance, self-respect, self-confidence, self-love, self-care, among others. These words describe how we feel about ourselves, think about ourselves and are shown by how we treat ourselves. They may seem like they are blending as we learn, soon you will see the different perceptions, unique meanings, and the purpose of them being set up this way. Out of them all, self-worth is the most important one of them all.

On the other hand, self-value is "more behavioral than emotional, more about how you act toward what you value, including yourself, than how you feel about yourself compared to others" (Stosny, 2014).

Similarly, the World Book Dictionary definition of self-esteem is "thinking well of oneself; self-respect," while self-worth is defined as "a favorable estimate or opinion of oneself; self-esteem" (Bogee, Jr., 1998).

Clearly, many of these terms are used to talk about the same ideas, but for those deeply immersed in these concepts, there is a slight difference. Dr. Christina Hibbert explains this:

"Self-esteem is what we think and feel and believe about ourselves. Self-worth is recognizing 'I am greater than all of those things.' It is a deep knowing that I am of value, that I am loveable, necessary to this life, and of incomprehensible worth." (2013).

Self-worth remains at the core of our thoughts, feelings, and behaviors. Which ultimately determines how we view our worthiness and value as a human being.

Self-Worth Theory?

The self-worth theory posits that an individual's main priority in life is to find self-acceptance that self-acceptance is often found through achievement (Covington & Beery, 1976). In turn, achievement is often found through competition with others. In conclusion, competing with others help us feel as if we have impressive achievements. Those achievements make us feel proud to be ourselves while enhancing our acceptance of ourselves.

The theory shows there are four main elements of the self-worth model:

- Ability;
- Effort;
- Performance
- Self-worth.

The first three, when in relation with one another, determine your level of self-worth. Ability and effort help to determine how an impact on performance and all three contribute to your feelings from worth and value. This is a simplified theory of how self-worth can be mistaken for just getting achievements. It is important to put the focus more so on healthy competing and "winning" against others. There are quite a few things that contribute to our self-worth.

While this hypothesis speaks to a decent comprehension of self-esteem as we will in general experience it, sadly, we place such a great amount of emphasis on our accomplishments. Beside contending and "winning" against others, numerous components can add to our ability to be self-aware worth.

Self-worth is determined by our abilities and our performance in the activities we deem valuable.

There are other ways to measure our self-worth, listed below are the most commonly used ones we use to compare our worth with the worth of others:

- Appearance
- Net Worth
- Status based on your social circle or the VIPs you know
- What you do for a living, career-wise
- Achievements

There are a ton of misunderstandings and misperceptions about self-worth, here are some factors that should not determine your self-worth:

Your To-Do List: Finishing your to-do list may feel amazing, but doing so does not equate to your worth as a human being.

Your Job: The only thing that matters with your job is whether or not it fulfills you and if you are good at it.

Social Media Status: Other people's opinions about your looks, status, or perspective do not affect your value.

Your Age: Age is created by man. It doesn't define whether you are or too old or too young for anything. Your age as a number does not factor into your self-value.

Other people: other people's opinions of you are none of your business, what they think, done, accomplished. Your personal satisfaction is more important than the thoughts, sayings, or beliefs of others.

Physical abilities such as running: How far you ran, the time you did it in, and who you beat doesn't matter. Whether it is something you enjoy or not, your ability in it does not determine your worth.

Grades: considering we are all unique individuals means we all have different strengths and weaknesses. We learn differently, so some of us just not fit for the classroom. The value of a straight-A student is the same as that of an F-student. The number of friends you have: The quality of friendships is better than the quantity. Either way, your value does not come from the number of connections we have.

Relationship status: people who place value into a committed relationship lack self-worth. Whether you are committed dating or single, none alter your self-worth.

Money: whether there is a ton in the bank or lack of, the maximal money you need for survival is $0.

Personal perks: from you amazing taste, sophistication, or having an eye for fine details, your worth remains the same.

You are the only one who determines yourself worth, there is a reason it has self in front of it. Whatever you believe, you can achieve.

No worries if you haven't quite reached this stage in your life yet, there are things you can do to define your self-worth

along with value yourself more. Let's discuss the ways to find fulfillment and feel complete as the extraordinary human being that you are. We are all worthy of unconditional love and respect.

The way we develop most lifestyle traits starts in childhood. Adolescents experience a lot of changes that cause pressure that ultimately affects their self-worth. It is important for them to focus on their value based upon their being instead of what they are doing. Show them value based upon who they are, not what they do by encouraging them, understanding them, and accepting them for who they are.

Researchers at Michigan State University gives to strategies for this to be effective:

1. Give unconditional positive regards, respect, and love.
2. Give them healthy opportunities to experience success (Clark-Jones, 2012). There are several people who play a part in showing teenagers their value from parents, family members, close friends, teachers, mentors, etc. Think about it, if you start off in the younger years showing teenagers you appreciate them for exactly who they are, they will learn it isn't necessary to achieve anything to earn your love. This takes away the risk of them putting made-up parameters on their self-love and respect.

Any way you can incorporate successful experiences in the younger people's lives encourages them to take on healthy risk with the successes that follow. To build a healthy sense of self-worth, expose them to opportunities where they can succeed. They have to go through these experiences on their own to feel worthy and valuable with minimal help from you, if any. Telling a person what they are never registers with people as much as it does with showing them. With adults, it is somewhat the same but slightly different.

Increasing self-worth and self-value in adults

Let's discuss how we can increase these key things within adults.

As adults, we need reminders of what does not determine our self-worth. Refer to the list because it is easy for us to get caught up into things that do not matter, especially when you are surrounded by people who value these things. Society puts unhealthy ideas of what self-value and self-worth are. Every now and then, take a step back to focus on the things that actually matter. Focus on being kind, showing compassion, having empathy, and respect for one another because these determine people's self-worth.

We all have an inner critic voice set up to work against us. Challenge this voice, identifying it as not your inner citric in situations that require you to externalize. Once we identify this voice as our own consistently, then the inner critic wins and you are doomed to always thinking the worse of yourself.

When your inner critic shows up, take a moment to reflect. Pause and ask yourself are these things based on facts. Is it being kind in doing so or telling you anything you need to know? If not, take control and say what the actual facts are out loud. Then look into the mirror and tell her she's dismissed. Sometimes you can avoid getting to this point by stopping to ask yourself what you will think next and pretend as if you can watch the next thought in your head...usually, nothing comes because you have separated yourself from your thoughts, and by acknowledging this, you have more control over your mind.

Whether you have self-worth reflects in your relationships.

People with low self-esteem base their self-worth on one thing in their lives, the relationships they have. As human beings, we love to be loved naturally, this feeling makes us feel better about ourselves. However, we have to work on feeling good about ourselves regardless if we are in a relationship or not.

If you are noticing that you are defining yourself based on the relationships in your life, then acknowledge that the love of another person doesn't define you nor your value. Taking time out to show yourself self-acceptance and self-compassion shows you that you are worthy of love and respect. This applies to every individual, whether you are in a relationship or not.

My confusion of what love is led me to a co-dependent relationship and allowance of someone else to define who I am, when all was said and done, I was forced to rediscover my sense of worth from scratch, which made the grief much harder than it should have been. You'll notice the difference in your relationships when you have a healthy sense of self-worth, your relationships will be better. My parents couldn't love me because they didn't love themselves. Upon learning this, I set out on a journey to reconnect with what love truly is. Speaking from experience, when you learn to love yourself, your ability to love others increases. If your relationships in your life seem unsatisfying, unloving, and unstable, there is a lack of self-respect. People with self-respect know their worth, have high self-esteem, and are happy with themselves. You feel whole whether in a relationship or not. This leads to two people in a relationship full of self-worth and happiness from the core with having a brighter promising future.

Self-Worth Scale

I know the question on everyone's mind right about now is where to start. A good starting point is always to determine what your current level of self-worth is. Here is a scale to help.

The Contingencies of Self-Worth Scale, this scale was developed by researchers Crocker, Luhtanen, Cooper, and Bouvrette in 2003. It consists of 35 items that measure self-worth in seven domains. These seven domains, with an example item from each domain, are:

- Approval from others (i.e., I don't care if other people have a negative opinion of me);
- Physical appearance (i.e., my self-esteem is influenced by how attractive I think my face or facial features are);
- Outdoing others in competition (i.e., my self-worth is affected by how well I do when I am competing with others);
- Academic competence (i.e., I feel bad about myself whenever my academic performance is lacking);
- Family love and support (i.e., my self-worth is not influenced by the quality of my relationships with my family members);
- Being a virtuous or moral person (i.e., my self-esteem depends on whether I follow my moral/ethical principles);
- God's love (i.e., my self-esteem would suffer if I didn't have God's love).

Each item is rated on a scale from 1 (strongly disagree) to 7 (strongly agree). Once you have rated each item, sum the answers to the five items for each domain and divide the total by 5 for the sub-scale score.

To learn more about this scale or use it to determine your own self-worth, refer to
https://www.midss.org/sites/default/files/continge...

Developing your Self-Worth

According to author and self-growth guru Adam Sicinski, there are five exercises for developing and maintaining self-worth. He explains them in five stages, there is no specific order to this. People will move back and forth and sometimes come back to specific ones.

1. Increase Your Self-Understanding

Realizing what your identity is and what you need precedes choosing if you are commendable. Mindfulness prompts self-comprehension, which is a significant part of finding out about self-esteem.

Here is a straightforward psychological test to take a shot at expanding your comprehension of yourself:

- Imagine that all that you have is abruptly detracted from you (i.e., assets, connections, companionships, status, work/profession, achievements and accomplishments, and so on.);
- Ask yourself these inquiries:

a. What if all that I have was abruptly detracted from me?
b. What if all I had left was simply myself?
c. How would that cause me to feel?
d. What would I really have that would be of worth?

Think about your responses to these inquiries and check whether you can arrive at this resolution: "Regardless of what happens remotely and regardless of what's detracted from me, I'm not influenced inside."

Next, become acquainted with yourself on a more profound level with these inquiries:

a. Who I am? I am . . . I am not . . .
b. How am I?
c. How am I on the planet?
d. How do others see me?
e. How do others talk about me?
f. What key life minutes characterize who I am today?
g. What presents to me the most enthusiasm, satisfaction, and delight?

Once you comprehend what your identity is and what satisfies and fulfills you, it's an ideal opportunity to see what isn't so incredible or simple about being you. Ask yourself these inquiries:

a. Where do I battle most?
b. Where do I have to improve?
c. What fears regularly keep me down?
d. What constant feelings hurt me?
e. What botches do I make?
f. Where do I reliably allow myself to go?

Finally, pause for a minute to take a gander at the flipside; ask yourself:

a. What capacities do I have?
b. What am I great at?

Spend time working through these steps, especially on the ones that a constant reminder of your self-worth and self-value.

Remember: What you do and how you do something is both completely different from who you truly are.

2. Boost Your Self-Acceptance

When you have a superior thought of what your identity is, the following stage is to improve your acknowledgment of yourself.

Start by pardoning yourself for anything you noted in thing 5 above. Think about any battles, requirements for development, errors, and unfortunate propensities you have, and focus on pardoning yourself and tolerating yourself without judgment or reasons. Consider all that you found out about yourself in the principal exercise and rehash these announcements:

- I acknowledge the great, the awful and the revolting;
- I completely acknowledge all aspects of myself, including my imperfections, fears, practices, and characteristics I probably won't be excessively glad for;
- This is the manner by which I am, and I am content with that

3. Enhance Your Self-Love

Once you put the work into accepting yourself for who you are, building love and caring for yourself becomes a lot easier. Make a habit out of extending yourself kindness, generosity, tolerance, and compassion.

While working on this daily goal pay attention to the language and tone you use with yourself in boosting your self-love. It is important to be positive, uplifting, and gentle with yourself when making this commitment.

As Sicinski mentioned, when in doubt on how to get started, you should think or say the things you are committing to aloud. Here are the simple statements he mentioned:

- I feel valued and special.
- I love myself wholeheartedly.
- I am a worthy and capable person.

4. Recognize Your Self-Worth

If you no longer want to base your self-worth on external factors, you must understand, accept, and love yourself. It is as simple as that.

Once you reach his point, it is important to appreciate everything about yourself by

recognizing your worth and appreciating yourself for the work you've done to get here, you must do the mental workouts in continuing to maintain your self-understanding, self-acceptance, self-love, and self-worth. As stated by Sicinski, To recognize your self-worth, remind yourself that:

- You no longer need to please other people;

- No matter what people do or say, and regardless of what happens outside of you, you alone control how you feel about yourself;
- You have the power to respond to events and circumstances based on your internal sources, resources, and resourcefulness, which are the reflection of your true value;
- Your value comes from inside, from an internal measure that you've set for yourself.

5. Take Responsibility for Yourself

You currently need to work on being liable for yourself, your conditions, and your issues.

Follow these rules proposed by proficient analyst to guarantee you are taking a shot at this activity in a solid manner:

- Take full obligation regarding all that transpires without parting with your own capacity and your organization;
- Acknowledge that you have the individual capacity to change and impact the occasions and conditions of your life.

Help yourself to remember what you have realized through these activities and realize that you hold the force in your own life. Revel in your all around earned ability to be self-aware worth and try to look after it.

Homework to help increase your Self-Worth

In case you're inclined toward filling in the spaces as opposed to finishing more freestyle activities and exercises, not to stress. Look at the four worksheets underneath that can assist you with building your self-esteem. About Me Sentence Finish

This worksheet diagrams a basic method to fabricate self-esteem. It just requires a pen or pencil and a couple of moments to finish. Use it for yourself or for your grown-up customers, however it was intended for kids and can be particularly compelling for them. This worksheet is just named "About Me: Sentence Finishing" and is actually what you may expect: it allows children to expound on themselves. In the event that your youth is too youthful to even think about writing down his own answers, sit with him and assist him with recording his reactions.

The sentence stems (or prompts) to finish include:

- I was truly glad when . . .
- Something that my companions like about me is . . .
- I'm pleased with . . .
- My family was glad when I . . .
- In school, I'm acceptable at . . .
- Something that makes me novel is . . .

Confidence Exam

This worksheet is useful for a wide crowd, including kids, teenagers, youthful grown-ups, and more seasoned grown-ups. The initial content shows that it's a confidence worksheet, however, the terms confidence and self-esteem are utilized reciprocally.

Finishing this worksheet will assist you with understanding your own feeling of getting, acknowledgment, regard, and love for yourself.

This sums up 15 proclamations and trains you to rate your faith in everyone on a scale from 0 (not in the slightest degree) to 10 (absolutely or totally). These affirmations are:

- I have confidence in myself;
- I am similarly as important as others;
- I would prefer to be me than another person;
- I am pleased with my achievements;
- I feel great when I get praises;
- I can deal with analysis;
- I am acceptable at tackling issues;
- I love attempting new things;
- I regard myself;
- I like the manner in which I look;
- I love myself in any event, when others reject me;
- I know my positive characteristics;

- I center around my victories and not my disappointments; I'm not reluctant to commit errors;
- I am glad to be me.
-

Include the entirety of the evaluations for these 15 explanations to get your absolute score, at that point rate your general self-appreciation regard on a scale from 0 (I totally disdain who I am) to 10 (I totally like who I am).

At last, react to the brief, "What might need to change with the end goal for you to climb one point on the rating scale? (i.e., for instance, on the off chance that you appraised yourself a 6 what might need to occur for you to be at a 7?)"

My Qualities and Characteristics

The "My Qualities and Characteristics" worksheet made by broad exploration from analyst is another open door for you or a youthful grown-up you know to take a shot at boosting self-getting, acknowledgment, love, and self-appreciation worth. It couldn't be simpler to finish—all you need is the worksheet, a pen or pencil, and a couple of moments.

For every one of the eight segments, there are three spaces to react; notwithstanding, in the event that you have multiple things to record, do as such.

The areas are:

- Things I am acceptable at;

- What I like about my appearance;
- I've helped other people by;
- What I esteem the most;
- Compliments I have gotten;
- Challenges I have survived;
- Things that make me interesting; and
- Times I've satisfied others.

A first date question: How aware are you of your traumas and suppressed emotions and tell me about how you are actively working to heal them before you try to project that shit on me.

13 Rules for dating when you struggle with self-worth.

- I do not want to be with anyone that doesn't want to be with me. I am not missing out. I will believe that. I will internalize that. I will live that.
- Their problem is their problem. I will focus on my own problems; my only responsibility is self-improvement.
- I will be single until I'm no longer AFRAID to be single.
- I BELIEVE I have self-worth, and so I have it.
- I will not be needy. People cannot appreciate things they haven't earned
- I am good by myself.

- I will constantly reinvest the anxiety over not being liked into liking myself.
- I will love myself. I will have standards. value myself above all else.
- The question will always be, are they worthy of me?
- The gap between what I feel I should do and what I know I should do is a knowledge gap. This is especially true in learning self-worth and my value in dating.
- FEELINGS ARE NOT FACTS.
- I need to live in reality, I have not properly adjusted to reality and I'm still in la la land, the land of what I wish would happen, not the real world of what's actually happening.
- I am fantastic. I am wonderful. I am loved. These are the facts.

There's no calculation for being a successful dater, however there is one thing you must have before an effective relationship: self-assurance. Dating is tied in with trusting you merit the best and you won't get much of anywhere without that conviction. Having low or no confidence can truly change your perspective of life in these manners:

- YOU LET GUYS TREAT YOU LIKE CRAP.
- YOU BELIEVE YOU DON'T DESERVE LOVE.
- YOU ALLOW YOUR FEAR OF REJECTION TO DICTATE YOUR LOVE LIFE.
- YOU LACK CONFIDENCE IN THE BEDROOM.

- YOU FORGET TO MAKE YOURSELF A PRIORITY.
- YOU FALL APART IF HE FALLS OUT OF LOVE.
- YOU BASE YOUR SELF-WORTH ON WHETHER OR NOT A GUY LIKES YOU.
- YOU WONDER WHY ANY GUY WOULD LOVE YOU.
- YOU ATTRACT NEGATIVE PARTNERS.
- YOU'LL NEVER BE HAPPY.

Satisfaction doesn't originate from your accomplice; it originates from you. On the off chance that you don't cherish yourself, at that point you're clearly not content with what your identity is. Prior to you even consider dating, not to mention being seeing someone, some an ideal opportunity to take a shot at confidence. You have to figure out how to be cheerful being you. Until you discover certainty and genuine affection for yourself, you're in an ideal situation being single.

After researching this, here are the most common things women who value their self-worth do differently in relationships

When you have poor self-worth, you get trapped in toxic relationships and sabotage new relationships which causes us to feel broken, devastated, and confused once the relationship ends.

Let's be clear having high self-esteem doesn't guarantee a happy relationship, however it does prepare you with the skills needed to identify what you want and what you deserve to have, as well as the strength to walk away from anything less than. Here are the most common things people with high self-esteem do differently in their relationships:

1. Confident ladies don't consider on the off chance that he enjoys them – they know he does.
2. Confident individuals acknowledge whether a relationship self-destructs, this is on the grounds that it wasn't right.
3. Confident ladies set sound limits (boundaries).
4. Confident ladies believe in themselves and the choices they make.
5. Confident ladies don't flaunt or talk themselves up.
6. Confident ladies acknowledge responsibility.
7. Confident ladies take the relationship for what it is and needn't bother with it to be a sure way.
8. Confident ladies don't remain in terrible connections.
9. Confident ladies don't urgently look for comfort.
10. Confident ladies pick admirably.

CHAPTER 8

Am I Black Enough (Socially Awkward or Anxiety)

Your greatest danger is ignorance of yourself.

Socially Awkward or Anxiety – Mental health conditions can make you more insecure and less confident when meeting new people.

You can't control other people's reactions to you, but you can control yourself with self-awareness. Our thoughts and feelings seem real to us, so we conclude they must be. Self-awareness impacts our social effectiveness.

It is all in your head literally and has nothing to do with your abilities.

When you are in comfortable situations and have to do things out of your comfort zone with a friend, the situation is different, why is that. Sometimes it is calming to feel safe around the people you are around because you're not inside your head as much. Think about the last time you went out with a best friend or took a trip with one...do you remember any anxious feelings? I doubt it.

Unspoken weapons for muted wars when your mind is being a battlefield.

Do You Have A Social Anxiety Disorder, Or Are You Just Socially Awkward?

We all have been at a point where we have said or did something awkward in front of other people. However, if you feel as if your awkwardness is tied to social anxiety, that's a different issue. Trust me, you are not alone.

Everybody has presumably said or accomplished something remarkable before others sooner or later in their lives, yet on the off chance that you have a feeling that your clumsiness is attached to social tension, that is an entire other issue. Also, you're not by any means the only one in that vessel.

Matt Lundguist, LCSW, a psychotherapist based in New York City, says his practice receives a lot of calls from potential patients who have either diagnosed themselves with social anxiety disorder, or who think they might have symptoms. If you think you might have social anxiety, it might comfort you to know that it's fairly common — according to the Anxiety and Depression Association of America (ADAA), this affects almost 15 million Americans, and is known as the second most commonly diagnosed anxiety disorder following specific phobias.

As common as it is, not every awkward interaction equates to you having social anxiety. When a person suffers from social anxiety disorder, being exposed to social situations or experiences with situations where they have to perform (like giving a speech) triggers anxiety and can even provoke panic attacks. And as Lundquist says, this is different from simply feeling like you're awkward when communicating to people.

"Some people just don't feel good at social situations, but [those situations] don't necessarily produce anxiety," he says. "That's the difference between social anxiety and social awkwardness."

However, social anxiety and social awkwardness are not different entities. Lundquist says that social anxiety disorder can sometimes stem from feeling unskilled socially, or like you don't fit in. I've always been known as a social butterfly and been equipped to handle social interactions from catching up with friends, meeting new people, giving speeches, or acting. However, I still have my moments of not being able to decide if I am coming from a place of fear or excitement in certain social situations. The outcome is ultimately the same when I am in my own head too much.

Social anxiety disorder can sometimes stem from feeling unskilled socially or like you don't fit in.

"If people have had humiliating experiences, or experiences of being abused or emotionally harmed in social contexts, then that can express itself as social anxiety, fear and avoidance of social context," Lundquist says.

Social anxiety disorder, he says, is defined by fearing social situations and avoiding them, with the avoidance being the key part. Other signs? When walking into a social situation, you can have signs of strong physical symptoms. These symptoms include having a rapid heart rate, nausea, sweating and even a panic attack (Lundquist says that a person does not necessarily have to experience all the symptoms listed to have a social anxiety disorder).

According to the ADAA, the problem is when those symptoms hinder a person living their lives — for example, someone may turn down job opportunities that require them to constantly interact with new people or even miss out on opportunities for human connection by avoiding a large group of friends. "If people are avoiding certain kinds of social situations, that speaks to an underlying anxiety," Lundquist says.

Fortunately, there are plenty of effective treatments for social anxiety and they can vary from person to person. Overall usually involve cognitive behavioral therapy, and addressing any possible trauma that could be the root of the issue. At any given time, we all might feel awkward around other people for a lot of reasons, but if your discomfort in social situations gets to where it is interfering with your everyday life, check in with your doctor or some type of professional help.

It's human nature to feel nervous in certain social situations. For instance, whenever we are going on a first date or giving a presentation in front of others, this may cause that feeling of butterflies in your stomach. But in social anxiety disorder, which can also be known as social phobia, these everyday interactions cause a significant amount of anxiety, fear, self-consciousness and embarrassment because of the fear being judged by others.

In social anxiety disorder, fear and anxiety can lead to avoidance in a way that can cause constant disruptions in your life. Extreme stress has been known to affect your daily routine with work, school or other activities.

Social anxiety disorder is a chronic mental health condition. Doesn't have to seem drastic considering there are learning coping skills in psychotherapy and options to take medications. Either way, they both can help you get the confidence you need and gain improvement with your ability to interact with others.

Symptoms

When feeling shy or have discomfort leading to a certain situation, they do not always show signs of social anxiety disorder, especially with children. Everyone has a different comfort level with social situations. This is dependable on your personality traits and life experiences. And sometimes, it just comes down to some people being naturally reserved while others are more outgoing. That differs from the nervousness you get on a daily. Social anxiety disorders usually start when you are a teen, but also has been known to start in younger children as well as adults.

Emotional and behavioral symptoms

Signs and side effects of social nervousness issues can persist into the following:

- Fear of circumstances in which you might be judged
- Worrying about humiliating or embarrassing yourself
- Intense dread of associating or chatting with outsiders
- Fear that others will see you look restless
- Fear of physical side effects that may cause you shame, for example, becoming flushed, perspiring, shuddering or having a temperamental voice
- Avoiding getting things done or addressing individuals out of dread of humiliation
- Avoiding circumstances where you may be the focal point of consideration

- Having uneasiness fully expecting a dreaded movement or occasion
- Enduring a social circumstance with exceptional dread or nervousness
- Spending time after a social circumstance breaking down your exhibition and recognizing imperfections in your communications
- Expecting the absolute worst results from a negative encounter during a social circumstance.

Children express this differently. Their anxiety is surrounded around interacting with adults or peers and expressed by crying, having temper tantrums, clinging to parents or refusing to speak in social situations.

Then you have the people who experience intense fear and anxiety only when performing in public by something such as a speech but remain find in other types of social situations. Known as performance anxiety.

Physical signs and symptoms can sometimes accompany social anxiety disorder and may include:

- Blushing
- Fast heartbeat
- Trembling
- Sweating
- Upset stomach or nausea

- Trouble catching your breath
- Dizziness or lightheadedness
- Feeling that your mind has gone blank
- Muscle tension

When avoiding common social situations, this means you may have everyday experiences that may be hard to endure due to social anxiety disorder. These include:

- Interacting with unfamiliar people
- Attending social gatherings
- Going to work or school
- Starting conversations
- Making eye contact
- Dating
- Entering a room in which people are already seated
- Returning items to a store
- Eating in front of others
- Using a public restroom

However, social anxiety disorder symptoms may vary over time. They can be exacerbated if you are facing a lot of stressful demands. Believe it or not, avoiding social situations that may cause anxiety may feel good at the time, but you are only utilizing the bandage method. A temporary quick fix because without treatment your anxiety increases in the long term. It would be wise to see your doctor or mental health professional if you can relate to this.

Much the same as with numerous other psychological well-being conditions, social tension problem emerges from an intricate cooperation of organic and ecological variables.

Potential causes include

- Inherited attributes. Tension issues run in families. Nonetheless, it isn't completely certain which bit of this might be because of hereditary qualities and what amount is because of learned behavior.
- Cerebrum structure. A structure in the mind called the amygdala (uh-MIG-duh-luh) may assume a function in controlling the dread reaction. Individuals with an overactive amygdala may have an uplifted dread reaction, causing expanded uneasiness in social circumstances.
- Environment. Social nervousness problems might be an educated conduct — a few people may build up the condition after an undesirable or humiliating social circumstance. Additionally, there might be a relationship between social tension issues and guardians who either model restless conduct in social circumstances or are all the more controlling or overprotective of their youngsters.

Danger factors

A few components can build the danger of creating social nervousness problem, including:

- Family history. You're bound to create social tension issues if your natural guardians or kin have the condition.
- Negative encounters. Youngsters who experience prodding, harassing, dismissal, criticism or embarrassment might be more inclined to social nervousness issues. Moreover, other negative occasions throughout everyday life, for example, family struggle, injury or misuse, might be related with social tension issues.
- Temperament. Kids who are modest, bashful, pulled back or controlled when confronting new circumstances or individuals might be at more serious danger.
- New social or work requests. Social uneasiness issue side effects normally start in the high school years, however meeting new individuals, giving a conversation in broad daylight or making a significant work introduction may trigger manifestations unexpectedly.
- Having an appearance or condition that draws consideration. For instance, facial deformation, stumbling or tremors because of Parkinson's illness can build sentiments of hesitance and may trigger social nervousness issues in certain individuals.

Difficulties

Left untreated, social nervousness can run your life. Tensions can meddle with work, school, connections or happiness regarding life. Social nervousness issue can cause:

Low confidence

- Trouble being self-assured
- Negative self-talk
- Hypersensitivity to analysis
- Poor social abilities
- Isolation and troublesome social connections
- Low scholastic and work accomplishment
- Substance misuse, for example, drinking an excess of liquor
- Suicide or self-destruction endeavors

Other tension issues and certain other emotional wellness issues, especially significant burdensome issues and substance misuse issues, frequently happen with social nervousness problems.

Counteraction

It is extremely unlikely to foresee what will make somebody build up an uneasiness problem, however you can find a way to decrease the effect of indications in case you're restless:

- Get help early. Nervousness, in the same way as other psychological well-being conditions, can be more earnestly to treat on the off chance that you stand by.
- Keep a diary. Monitoring your own life can support you and your emotional wellness proficient distinguishes what's causing you stress and what appears to assist you with feeling good.

- Prioritize issues throughout your life. You can diminish uneasiness via cautiously dealing with your time and energy. Invest energy doing things you appreciate.
- Avoid undesirable substance use. Liquor and medication use and even caffeine or nicotine use can cause or intensify uneasiness. In case you're dependent on any of these substances, stopping can make you restless. On the off chance that you can't stop all alone, see your primary care physician or discover a treatment program or care group to support you.

Accepted practices and prompts, for example, realizing when to make proper acquaintance or giving individuals individual space, assist you with exploring social circumstances. You may have been legitimately shown a portion of these standards. Others, you might've gotten on by watching others.

When it comes to witnessing someone struggling with one of these norms, it is natural to want to cringe internally and feel embarrassed for the other person. It is easy to identify these things because of the way we feel when it is us. We tend to feel our stomachs flipping and turning. Especially when it comes to fumbling over something as simple as an introduction to someone new or tripping over your words.

Social awkwardness doesn't have to have a bad connotation behind it, especially since it can benefit you in ways. With that said, it still doesn't make it any less distressing in the moment.

Overall research gives us a look into signs of social awkwardness, tips for overcoming it, and reasons it might not be such a negative thing.

How do I know if I'm socially awkward?

Social awkwardness is definitely not a psychological well-being issue — there's no analytic rules or even a solid definition. It's even more an inclination, or an assortment of sentiments and encounters that structure an example in your life.

These sentiments and encounters frequently result from:

- failure to see certain expressive gestures
- misunderstanding or not seeing others' non-verbal communication

Heidi McKenzie, PsyD, explains that socially awkward people might have a hard time navigating conversations or working their way into a group. As a result, they might seem a bit "off" to others.

It's difficult to perceive social clumsiness in yourself since you probably won't know about a portion of the expressive gestures you aren't getting on. Rather, you may very well notification you don't appear to fit in with your companions. Social ponderousness, in itself, is definitely not an awful thing.

Be that as it may, it can get hazardous in the event that it prompts trouble due to:

- people offering harsh comments
- spending a ton of time contemplating whether you've accomplished something incorrectly
- frequently experiencing difficulty in social circumstances
- wanting to make companions yet attempting to associate with others

- feeling dismissed by others

Ideally, everybody would perceive that individuals are interesting and have distinctive ranges of abilities. However, in all actuality, this doesn't generally occur.

This can be hard to confront. However, it doesn't mean you have to change what your identity is. Social circumstances may not be your zone of solidarity, however there are things you can do to limit your worry around these situations.

CHAPTER 9

Feel the Fear and do it anyway (Reconnecting with yourself)

Don't feel bad for outgrowing people who had a chance to grow with you.

— Tim Karsliyev?

I was starting to notice my growth due to less and less I was starting to have in common with the people in my circle, which had gotten smaller throughout this journey. The more self-aware I became, the fewer connections I would have with other people. I didn't enjoy small talk anymore. I was looking for connections on deeper levels for deeper intellectual discussions. It was too late for me to turn back, considering I've already taken the "red pill" filled with unpleasant truths.

The anthropologist and ethicist Dawn Prince-Hughes argues that the standards of personhood include self-awareness, ability to understand complex emotions, and a capacity for empathy. Sometimes seeing people at the mental capacity you're at could cloud your judgment. Trust yourself and know that sometimes-other people grow as well. What happens when you continue to see people at the level they used to be. As human beings, we all make mistakes, change, grow, and sometimes life has a way of shaping us into a different person. Reconnections can be healthy when life experiences put you through lessons learned you can develop empathy for the next person and stop making it about yourself.

Reasons you don't want to reconnect may be your own lack of forgiveness with the situation and its effects, not the person.

Sometimes it is good to look at your foundation...family. They determine how you view the other relationships in your life.

Just like your immediate family is the foundation you base your friendships on depending on your birth order and relationships with your siblings. The same goes for your parents when it comes to deciding the person you marry.

People with stronger personal relationships feel connected to someone or something other than themselves. A solid foundation of healthy friendships gives you something to hold on to during difficult and stressful times that can often lead to unhealthy actions and patterns.

The overall common conclusion based on many theories is that, a portion of the essential needs of youth are love and passionate association. At the point when we get these, we figure out how to feel commendable and adorable. A large number of us grow up without these requirements being sufficiently met. This absence of association can have broad physical and mental ramifications for us.

Not encountering a caring association as a youngster can prompt inclination and a profound longing in adulthood. Sadly, attempting to get this connection from others, as opposed to figuring out how to interface with ourselves as well as other people, can prompt numerous individual and relationship issues.

Following my certifications in different aspects surrounding mental health, I've been able to work with a few clients. I now see the importance of my focus for helping others first connect with themselves -- with their feelings and their higher self/personal source of spiritual guidance.

Here's why:

1. An Inner Black Hole vs. Inner Fulfillment

At the point when separated from ourselves - from who we truly are and from our emotions - and when we are not filling ourselves with adoration through our otherworldly association, we make a dark gap inside. The dark opening we've made through our self-relinquishment becomes like a vacuum, attempting to pull love from others. This destitution drives individuals away, so we feel much more disliked. At the point when we need obligation regarding our own prosperity and we open to finding out about cherishing ourselves, we make the way for interfacing with an unbounded wellspring of adoration. Figuring out how to bring this affection inside and share it with others makes profound inward satisfaction.

2. Failed Relationships vs. Sharing Love

Since we meet up at our regular degree of self-surrender and our normal degree of self-esteem, in the event that we are relinquishing ourselves by detaching from ourselves and dodging obligation regarding our sentiments, we will probably draw in somebody doing likewise. Each accomplice trusts that the other will fill the dark opening inside. While they may appear to do this for one another for a brief timeframe, Inevitably, each feels disliked and angry, prompting relationship disappointment. We can't top off someone else. We each need to do this for ourselves, and afterward share our affection with one another. We can't interface on a profound degree of adoration with one another when we are not associated with ourselves.

I would say, imparting adoration to another who is additionally topped off with affection and sharing it, is the most satisfying and euphoric involvement with life. Try not to mistake getting love for sharing affection - they are light years separated!

3. Depression and Loneliness vs. Happiness and Joy

Sorrow is an enormous issue in our general public. While there are numerous foundations for sentiments of melancholy, one of the causes is separation from self - self-relinquishment. Similarly as a youngster gets discouraged when the parent is detached and inaccessible, so our internal identity - our inclination self - gets discouraged when we are disengaged from our sentiments and not assuming cherishing liability for them. Another reason for discouraged emotions is social disengagement and the subsequent dejection, which is frequently one consequence of separating from ourselves and afterward being not able to associate with others.

The film Upbeat goes on us on an outing the world over to the most joyful individuals on earth. Constantly, these are individuals who live in networks where they feel associated with one another. They have a sense of security since they look out for one another.

They are not desolate.

Notwithstanding, numerous individuals who have attempted to build up associated or deliberate networks leave them for a similar explanation as to why they leave relationships: They don't work except for if individuals are connected with themselves and assume responsibility for their own emotions.

4. Physical Illness vs. Physical Health

Stress is a significant reason for sickness (see The Science of Conviction by Dr. Bruce Lipton). At the point when we carry on with our carries on with disengaged from ourselves - not tuning in to and taking adoring consideration of our emotions - and separated from our own wellspring of direction, love and solace, we can't oversee pressure well. Self-deserting itself causes a lot of tension and stress, which enacts the battle or-flight reaction and adversely influences our safe framework.

There is some sign, as per Malcolm Gladwell in Anomalies, that individuals who live in associated networks are far more advantageous than the individuals who live in a more secluded manner. Association with self as well as other people is indispensable for acceptable wellbeing.

5. Addictions vs. Self-Regulation

At the point when we have not figured out how to associate with our thoughts and with the admiration and support of our profound direction, we frequently go to addictions as a method of overseeing excruciating emotions. To have the option to oversee and direct our emotions in sound manners, we have to associate them with a craving to assume appreciating obligation for them. Going to addictive conduct is a type of self-relinquishment - a method of keeping away from duty regarding our sentiments - and can prompt many negative results.

6. Violence vs. Compassion

At the point when we have not figured out how to completely feel our agonizing emotions, humanely overseeing them, gaining from them and afterward delivering them, we may put some distance between our humankind. It is the powerlessness to oversee torment that can prompt damaging and pointless conduct. At the point when we can't interface with and feel empathy for our own emotions, we may lose our capacity to feel sympathy for other people. At the point when this happens, we can carry on in brutally destructive manners.

7. Boredom vs. Passion and Creativity

Our enthusiasm and inventiveness flourish through our association with our sentiments and with our otherworldly direction. At the point when we separate from our emotions to secure against torment, we likewise shut out bliss, innovativeness and enthusiasm. Life turns out to be level, futile and exhausting. Love and happiness live in a similar spot in the heart as depression and disaster. At the point when we shut down, attempting to not feel our dejection and tragedy, we additionally shut down our capacity to feel love and delight. This is a dismal method to live.

You don't need to live thusly. You can figure out how to bond from inside. You can figure out how to move your concentration from external - attempting to get love and association from others - to internal, genuinely cherishing yourself as well as other people. You can figure out how to move from abstaining from feeling your difficult emotions to sympathetically grasping them with a longing to find out about what they are letting you know. You can figure out how to take cherishing care of yourself and experience the profound delight of offering your adoration to other people.

I don't generally experience the ill effects of gloom, yet I certainly have my minutes when I'm feeling sad. Once in a while this is on the grounds that I'm managing troublesome issues, or life is simply not going my direction. Different occasions, it's difficult to pinpoint where my trouble originates from. I am typically a playful individual, these circumstances leave me depleted and tired, with no energy to do anything I don't completely need to do. I simply need to be separated from everyone else.

In any case, that never causes me to feel better.

The explanation is that we as a whole need to feel connected. Study after investigation reports that as social creatures, people need one another. We have to feel upheld, esteemed, and adored. Those with great connections are more joyful, more beneficial, and live longer than the individuals who report feeling desolate.

At the point when I think about my own encounters, it's astonishing how associating with somebody, even quickly, can give me what I have to officer on. For instance, there are times I've felt as portrayed above, and have been sulking around at home. My telephone rings. My motivation is to not respond to it, however for reasons unknown I do, and I hear an old buddy's voice on the opposite end. She's simply calling to make a proper acquaintance. We talk about nothing significant for around five minutes, guarantee to get together soon, and state our farewells.

My spirits have been lifted. I even grin as I remember something my companion and I just kidded about. I push myself and I escape from the house to go for a stroll. A few people grin at me as we pass, and I grin back. I give compliments to a bystander on her shoes and stop to pet somebody's puppy. When I show up home, I am feeling far superior than I had been feeling before my telephone rang.

We regularly consider interacting with others as having sincere talks where we share our most profound contemplations and feelings or open up about difficult to-examine sentiments or occasions in our lives. This is unquestionably interfacing and is significant for us all of us do on occasion.

Be that as it may, associations can likewise be as straightforward as my walk. A wonderful cooperation with a store assistant, a mutual roar with laughter, even an instant message to a relative, can all, somewhat, fulfill our inborn requirement for networking. Unfortunately, huge numbers of us have completely decreased human interactions for associations with virtual ones. We rack up companions on Facebook and join a wide range of virtual local gatherings. We shop on the internet, restricting those lovely connections with store representatives referenced previously. We frequently value our autonomy, on zeroing in exclusively on our own goals and wants, and on not requiring any other person. This direction may lead us to just focusing on our own objectives, for example, a productive career, which may leave us feeling neglected also.

I'm not saying we shouldn't make a solid effort to focus on our objectives. There should be a balance. In carrying on with our lives and seeking after our fantasies, we have to perceive how significant fundamental human associations are a part of human nature with a positive outcome. When we understand this, we can intentionally pursue making these associations that make certain to improve our lives. Furthermore, it very well might be as straightforward as going outside for a walk.

We as a whole realize that soothing feeling when we are truly grasped – feeling heard, genuinely comprehended and upheld by another person. That warm sentiment of human association is so significant in keeping up our general passionate and physical wellbeing. Many studies have demonstrated that individuals who have fulfilling connections are more joyful, have less medical conditions, and live more. On the other hand, a general absence of social ties is related with wretchedness and later-life intellectual decay, just as with expanded mortality and why understanding human association is so significant.

What is Human Connection?

Human association is an energy trade between individuals focusing on each other. It has the ability to extend the occasion, rouse change and assemble trust.

What is Social Connection?

When researchers refer to the concept of "social connection," they mean the feeling you belong to a group and generally feel close to other people. Scientific evidence strongly suggests this is a core psychological need essential to feeling satisfied with your life.

Emma Seppala of the Stanford Center for Compassion and Altruism Research and Education, and author of the 2016 book "The Happiness Track," wrote, "People who feel more connected to others have lower levels of anxiety and depression. Studies show they also have higher self-esteem, greater empathy for others, are more trusting and cooperative and, as a consequence, others are more open to trusting and cooperating with them.

Brene Brown, a professor at the University of Houston Graduate College of Social Work, specializes in social connection, said in an interview that "A deep sense of love and belonging is an irresistible need of all people. We are biologically, cognitively, physically, and spiritually wired to love, to be loved, and to belong. When those needs are not met, we don't function as we were meant to." We may think we need cash, power, distinction, excellence, endless youth or another vehicle, yet at the base of the majority of these wants is a need to have a place, to be acknowledged, to associate with others and to be cherished.

What are the Benefits of Social Connections?

Flexibility, the capacity to bounce back after distressing circumstances, is encouraged when you give and get uphold. Building positive associations with individuals can have any kind of effect in how strong you are. Attempt to associate with individuals who have an inspirational viewpoint and can make you snicker and help you. The surer your connections are, the better you can confront life's difficulties.

What is Social Isolation?

Social Detachment is a condition of complete or close total absence of contact between an individual and society. It varies from depression, which mirrors an impermanent absence of contact with different people.

"Social isolation is far and away the strongest social risk factors out there," said Steve Cole, a genetics researcher at the University of California Los Angeles.

Depression and social separation negatively affect the human body. These can subvert the prosperity of essentially every real framework, including the cerebrum. Studies show that individuals who are persistently forlorn have fundamentally more coronary illness, are more defenseless against metastatic malignancy, have an expanded danger of stroke and are bound to create neurodegenerative maladies, for example, Alzheimer's.

Abandoned grown-ups are 25 percent bound to pass on carelessly. Old individuals who are neglected kick the bucket at double the rate as the individuals who are socially associated. All of which makes the spike in dejection in American culture much all the more disturbing. Analysts gauge that around 60 million Americans — one-fifth of the populace — experience the ill effects of the torment of depression. Furthermore, with a large number of people born after WW2 currently confronting a profoundly contracting social world, the rising tide of dejection has all the signs of a boundless and expensive pandemic. We have gotten a taste of this with COVID-19.

Why does loneliness 'feel' so bad?

For those who doubt, just think of the sting of rejection. A brain imaging study led by Ethan Kross at the University of Michigan suggests that the same parts of the brain are activated during social rejection as during physical pain. Another recent study led by Shelley Taylor at the University of California Los Angeles suggests that stress due to conflict in relationships leads to increased inflammation levels in the body. Both physically and psychologically, we experience social connection as positive and rejection or loneliness as negative.

According to Matthew Lieberman, a professor at UCLA, the importance of social connection is so strong that when we are rejected or experience other social pain, our brains "hurt" as they do when we feel physical pain. "Social and physical pain are more similar than we imagine," Lieberman said. "We don't expect someone with a broken leg to 'just get over it.' Yet when it comes to the pain of social loss, this is a common, and mistaken response." The bottom line: We need to take social pain just as seriously as we do physical pain.

How can we build stronger social connections?

Data indicates that we can increase social connections through practicing compassion for others as well as for ourselves.

Another approach to construct more grounded social associations is to ask yourself what might fulfill you in adding to your locale. Zeroing in on "what you can provide for other people" is a demonstrated method to feel both better about yourself and more associated with others. Correspondingly, you can contribute by instructing yourself on side interests or a reason that is important to you. Search for clubs, associations, normal occasions, and projects associated with your neighborhood public venues, libraries and schools.

Ultimately and generally significant: Interfacing with Yourself

You should know what your identity is and believe in yourself on the off chance that you want to interface with others. On the off chance that you don't trust in what your identity is and where you need to lead, chip away at that before doing whatever else.

In a world brimming with individuals, what can be more delightful than realizing how to frame sound connections and build up further associations with everyone around us – to feel socially associated, particularly in the present progressively separated world. To get familiar with the intensity of human association, all are welcome to go to this free, sensational night as we center around interfacing with ourselves as well as other people.

"Never underestimate the empowering effect of human connection. All you need is that one person, who understands you completely, believes in you and makes you feel loved for what you are, to enable you - to unfold the miraculous YOU."

— Drishti Bablani, Wordions

Meeting individuals and winning their trust is fundamental to business achievement and life achievement.

Conclusions communicated by Business person benefactors are their own.

We are intrinsically social animals, designed to search each other out and significantly molded by our connections and unions.

Our capacity to relate to each other and convey our considerations and thoughts separates us and makes us interestingly human. We normally look for more profound relationships with individuals as a method of distinguishing and getting others and ourselves. However, it's not in every case simple to make those associations. The bonds we make are critical to building our organizations and making full and cheerful lives. Notwithstanding, in a bustling world brimming with interruptions, it's difficult to fabricate companionships, particularly when we have restricted time.

Here are some ways you can build deeper connections with anyone you meet.

1. Pay attention.

At the point when somebody is conversing with you, it's significant that you truly center around what they're stating and focus on the subtleties they give. You can find out such a great amount about somebody just by tuning in to them and seeing both their verbal and nonverbal correspondence.

Checking your telephone or filtering the space to see who to converse with next is discourteous and pretentious and shows you couldn't care less about what the other individual is stating. Visually connect. Pose inquiries. Zero in on becoming acquainted with the other individual, regardless of whether you just have a restricted chance to talk.

2. Make a good first impression.

Non-verbal communication is personally attached to how others see you and their initial introductions of you. How you hold yourself, your stance and your outward appearances are signs others will take a gander at to evaluate what kind of individual you are and whether you are congenial and affable. Know about your demeanors, manner of speaking and signals.

Do you visually connect all through a discussion, showing interest? Or on the other hand do you keep your arms collapsed before you, shaping a boundary? Recall that nonverbal correspondence is similarly as significant as the words you use.

3. What's my name?

Not every person is skilled at putting names to appearances, and it very well may be especially hard to recollect names on the off chance that you are in a social setting where you're meeting many individuals in a short measure of time. Yet, recollecting individuals' names and tending to them straightforwardly will right away cause them to feel recognized and invited.

At the point when you meet individuals unexpectedly, have a go at saying their name a few times during your discussion and acquainting them with others. For instance: "Ideal to meet you, Tim. Have you met JoAnne?" The more occasions you state their name, the simpler it will be to recall it.

Get some information about themselves. What are their interests or hobbies? Discover something that will help lock their name into your memory bank. Attempt to consider something amusing or significant to connect with them or utilize a mental helper to recollect their name (e.g., Carlos from California or Brandy with the bounced hair style).

4. Have a connection story.

Make yourself lively by having a tale about yourself that gives understanding into what your identity is and what you're about. In case you're a yearning business visionary, create a story regarding why this is imperative to you and what encounters have filled your wants and life objectives.

Your association story ought to be explicit and incorporate into the occasions with others. It ought to be significant and give individuals a window into your convictions and inspirations. It ought to likewise cause others to feel good offering their stories to you.

Use narrating to give individuals a brief look into what your identity is and what you accept.

Stories catch individuals' consideration more than running through dry realities and data.

5. Add value.

Make yourself important and individuals will value you. Being of administration to other people, even in little ways, is an extraordinary method to associate.

Perhaps you have a tip on a job that will be coming open, or possibly you realize somebody searching for administrations they offer. It could be something as little as loaning them a book or informing them regarding an extraordinary TED talk or YouTube video on a point they are keen on. Figure out how to grasp liberality and you will make yourself as well as other people more fruitful.

6. Do your research.

In the event that having spur of the moment discussion make your palms sweat and prompts you to run for the entryway, consider doing a little preparation early. Thoroughly considering a few inquiries to pose to individuals will help set your psyche straight and mitigate nervousness.

The objective isn't to have a rundown of inquiries you can pull out and recount. A little prep work will assist you with feeling certain and loose so you can have a free-flowing discussion. Before you go to a social gathering or work-related event, create three open-finished or interesting questions to help keep your discussion moving.

Ensure they aren't excessively intrusive toward the individual; in any case, they ought to be sufficiently attentive to make the individual consider their reaction. A more important and more profound discussion will cause you more noteworthy and help other people to feel a connection with you.

7. Spark interest with a conversation piece.

Once in a while everything necessary to captivate everyone is flaunting your exceptional personal style. Do you have a specific shading you like to wear? An fondness for bright tennis shoes? Or then again maybe you like wearing fashionable heels with your dress or jeans. Wearing something that can be a friendly exchange will assist you with appearing to be both receptive and interesting. Nonetheless, ensure that you aren't freeing yourself up to be the aim of jokes or turning individuals off with something conceivably hostile. Think about this as an opportunity to show a little energy, assist you with standing apart from the group and put a grin on individuals' appearances.

8. Wear your heart on your sleeve.

We as a whole have considerations, thoughts, convictions and objectives. Be eager to share a touch of yourself - what your identity is and what you put stock in - and others will normally be interested and need to draw in you. Have you carried on with an intriguing life or would you say you are energetic about a cause? Individuals will discover you additionally fascinating and vital on the off chance that they find out about your encounters and what really matters to you.

This doesn't mean you ought to consume discussions. Be mindful so as not to preach or talk to others on a motive or issue you care about. Essentially grasp your interests and offer them with others - it might be an incredible method to participate in more profound discussions or amicable discussions.

9. Be open to learning.

As extraordinary for what it's worth to share your background, recall no one enjoys a person who dominates the conversation. Continuously be available to hearing others' thoughts and stories. Offer the stage and fight the temptation to consistently attempt and "one up" somebody with your insight or ability.

You can separate barriers by hearing what another person needs to state. Odds are you don't really know it all and being available to hearing another perspective will reveal insight into something new.

10. Show you care.

Being authentic and giving sympathy and grace will never become unpopular, and costs you literally nothing. Show your appreciation to others by saying thank you and being appreciative to the individuals who help you. You can construct further associations with individuals essentially by showing your human side.

On the off chance that you are inspiring, positive and show normal kindness to people around you, you will fabricate bonds that go past business. Keep in mind the intensity of genuine companionships.

Make New Connections Anywhere You Go

There are many chances to meet new individuals and develop your expert organization consistently. In any case, a great many people depend on formal systems administration occasions to pull out their business cards and start discussions. Rather, make the most of more subtle chances.

An association can occur in the most improbable spots, merging while you're in line for your morning espresso, on a plane heading off to your next conference, throughout a break at a workshop, or at a party time occasion.

The principal rule of systems administration is perceivability. At the point when I began my business 6 years prior, I joined proficient associations, affiliations and different gatherings. However, that wasn't sufficient. I realized that I needed to get indispensable to get observed. As it were, you should see and be seen for others to know what your identity is.

Volunteer to serve on the leading group of a neighborhood philanthropic or go to good cause raising support occasions. Volunteer to give an introduction or visitor talk to sharpen your public talking abilities. Remember that you are your own best business card.

As you approach your day, keep your eyes and ears open for friendly exchanges. Search for chances to be in leadership. On the off chance that someone more interesting notices he is searching for a decent café, toll in and present yourself and propose a portion of your preferred spots to eat. Search for things you share for all intents and purpose, particularly shared encounters, to begin truly intriguing discussions.

It might appear to be strange from the start, however the more you practice, the more associations you'll make. Organizations develop exponentially. For each new association you make, you acquire those optional associations. It's a lot simpler to request an acquaintance than it is with cold pitch somebody or present yourself suddenly. Rather than trusting that an event will be organized, utilize these tips to begin a discussion with an outsider.

Give a strong handshake. Early introductions are incredible, and a decent handshake passes on certainty. Continuously stand when you shake somebody's hand since it shows regard for yourself and the other individual. As you offer your hand, visually connect, grin, say your first and last name, and something important to you.

Discover a connector. In case you're new at an occasion, ask somebody in control or somebody who knows many individuals to introduce you to others in their organization. A presentation from an insider can be more powerful than if you acquaint yourself with a gathering of outsiders.

Find an individual's hobbies and interests. You could state something like, "What things do you like to do in your extra time?"

Nobody likes to discuss work the entire night, so your new associate will value your authentic intrigue. It's consistently pleasant when somebody sets aside the effort to become acquainted with what your identity is, not exactly what you do.

Offer a genuine commendation. This can be an incredible method to start casual chat. Everybody adores a praise. At the point when somebody has won an honor or accomplished something critical at work, praise her on her business achievements.

Extras are protected friendly exchanges. Notice you like an individual's PC case, shoes, tie or purse.

Know a little about a ton of things. Keep awake to date on current issues. On the off chance that you are intrigued and fascinating, individuals will be attracted to you. At the point when you travel on business, snatch a neighborhood paper when you show up at the air terminal or inn. Acquaint yourself with nearby news and you'll generally have something to discuss. Avoid no-no themes including sex, cash, unseemly jokes and legislative issues. Stay in contact. After you meet new associations, make certain to develop them. Continuously trade business cards so you can interface on LinkedIn a while later. Send an email or a manually written note to tell the individual you delighted in meeting him. In the event that you go over a business opportunity or a news story you figure your new colleague may be keen on, let him know. At the point when you keep in contact, connections will normally develop. Remember, *no one actually has their shit together. We're all figuring it out one day at a time.*

CHAPTER 10

It is a Marathon not a Sprint (Enjoy the Process)

"The prize is in the process" – Baron Baptiste

A significant key to progress and a solid life is to live it up during the cycle of whatever you are attempting to achieve. Unfortunately, happiness is something that numerous individuals leave by the wayside—particularly when change is occurring at a colossal rate and the weight is on to rethink yourself and accomplish new objectives. More now than any other time in recent memory, individuals are experiencing issues adjusting their lives, and there simply doesn't appear to be sufficient opportunity to do everything. Feelings of anxiety can get excessively serious, and negative feelings such as self-question, overpower, outrage and dread can become hazardous outlooks. While never acknowledging it, individuals permit their capacity to have a good time become auxiliary when it's generally essential.

Studies have demonstrated the individuals who settle on cognizant decisions (and it is a decision) to have a ball and giggle for the duration of the day are more innovative, beneficial and strong to testing circumstances. They are additionally bound to effectively discover answers for complex issues. Zeroing in on your joy makes you more perceptive as well as changes creativeness into high gear. How wise and how awakened would you say you are?

Doesn't it simply bode well that in the event that you are appreciating the cycle of whatever you are attempting to accomplish, that the chances will be in support of yourself to remain inspired and arrive at the result you want? It just appears obviously evident to deliberately pick bliss, to feel great during the cycle.

Yet, I would bet any measure of cash that when working out their short or long haul objectives and plans, the vast majority don't count on having a good time during the cycle as a component of the condition. Rather, they fall prey to risky outlooks that decline their potential for joy.

They put their joy on pause when they rehash and disguise negative articulations like: "I'll have a ball when I take care of business," "I'll be upbeat when I'm valued," or "I'll be glad when I get more cash-flow." And I used to state this frequently: "I'll have a good time when I arrive at a specific status throughout everyday life."

Stunning! The weight we put on ourselves…

I see how simple it is for us to get so gotten up to speed in the buzzing about of attempting to get by we overlook what it resembles to live. At times life expends us to where we permit ourselves to get detained by our very own shows and become neglectful to all the positive qualities in our lives. Yet, who says we can't in any event attempt to obtain a more beneficial disposition and search for the delight in and around our difficulties and mishaps? Why not center around what's working, rather focusing on what isn't?

The uplifting news is there are in every case new chances to feel better and to be upbeat. Envision life resembles Bizarre Pivotal Situations where joyful occasions show up nonstop. Odds are, the chance to feel better and to be cheerful has just shown up. Some of the time it's directly before you. Out of the blue, you can't move your concentration to see and value it.

Despite what is happening around you, you can feel more joyful, you can be advantageous, influence in progress, and live it up during the phase. At the point when you move your concentration and the manner in which you think, your viewpoint changes. There is positively no explanation: you can't anticipate the future, define objectives, go through your everyday schedule, manage the unforeseen, and still settle on cognizant decisions to feel better and have a ball at the same time.

In the event that you do, you won't just produce the fuel that drives inspiration, however you will be changing that inspiration into high gear. Why? Since satisfaction is the sparkle that lights energy and excitement. Continuously recall that. Record it!

These two powers are vital to getting the things you want. Since the energy they transmit won't just increase your general level of consideration, they additionally produce a ground-breaking association with a higher piece of yourself. "Enthusiasm" originates from the Greek word "entheos"— which means the God inside.

At the point when you are really energetic and excited about your vision, you initiate this ground-breaking energy to aid in creating your fantasies. At the point when difficulties are out of control, it's energy and excitement that constrains you to grab your vision and pushes you to go that additional mile. It's energy and excitement that push you into a zone where you feel certain, courageous and successful.

Continuously sustain your energy and eagerness. Permit yourself to get amped up for it. Feel it, sense it, grasp it. Picture your objectives and dreams with it. Since when you intensely clutch your vision with energy and eagerness, you will encounter new conditions, openings and fortunate occasions.

We must learn to enjoy the process and stop worrying about the outcome

"Slow down and everything you are chasing will come around and catch you"

—John De Paula

Recall the Tasmanian Fiend?

That crazed animation character turning wild, colliding with everything in his way? Showing up suddenly. Leaving disorder afterward.

That was basically me and my way to deal with "living through my passions."

In the relatively recent past, I was truly attempting to achieve these things simultaneously. I've consumed my whole time on earth being intensely associated with a numerous amount of extracurricular activities, for example, educational things, self-improvement missions, career related things, leisure activities, trips, companions, family, connections, passive revenue, and so forth. Obviously, I was consistently in a hurry.

So how did that all work out, you might ask. Total disaster.

It turned into a problem of automated disruptions. An existence where quicker is better, performing multiple tasks is the public song of constancy, and innovation will liberate you to be more beneficial and make you more insightful.

Where you needn't bother with human association any longer. You can just "interface" to your worldwide crowd via technology, which was nearly equivalent to being there with them.

Then again, actually it's most certainly not.

I was tricked into trusting I could achieve so many more errands with this innovation and accomplish fantastic accomplishments by basically sitting before a PC screen.

I was additionally following a few effective bloggers and online advertisers and taking in all that I could from them. In any case, this just enhanced the fancy I could achieve every one of these things without a moment's delay since they had done it.

Just every one of those advertisers appeared to be exceptionally centered around only a certain something and they were doing it well. The issue for me was that I had numerous irons in numerous flames and none were getting exceptionally hot. I call this The Thrashing Impact.

In any case, to express gratitude toward God that some place amidst this disorder, I started rehearsing reflection. You could state I at long last recovered. I immediately eased back down and saw an alternate point of view. It didn't occur without any forethought. There were no structural movements in my insane way of life. I needed to get up significantly prior to now accommodate my reflection into my effectively crazy timetable.

In any case, it was the best thing I actually might have done.

Gradually, through the act of calming my psyche, I discovered clearness.

I unmistakably observed my connection to this urgent need to achieve something significant in this life and be perceived by the world for it; and how these outside achievements would some way or another approve me personally, like what my identity was at that point wasn't sufficient.

It didn't take much time before I noticed the madness in my behaviors.

I expected to characterize what I needed my life to represent. At that point I expected to wipe out everything else that didn't serve that end. Yet, the most significant revelation was figuring out how to at long last relinquish everything desired that any of these yearnings required to materialize. Or then again on the off chance that they were intended to be, I expected to quit stressing over when they would occur, which it turns out was an immense source of dissatisfaction.

Connection, stress, dissatisfaction—these things don't exist in nature. Things unfold as they should in nature.

Every now and then the downpours come. Once in a while they don't. Now and then one uproar can change the course of millions of lives in only a couple of moments.

A stream runs its course dependent on the lay of the land. At the point when it meets an impediment, it doesn't battle with it. It just circumvents it… in the end.

What amount of time it requires is of little outcome. After about 6,000,000 years or thereabouts, it may cut something as glorious as the Stupendous Gorge. No one's watching the check in nature.

A tree is cheerful any place it develops. It doesn't subtly wish to grow legs and run off to some other additionally happening aspect of the woodland. (Robert Ice composed a truly extraordinary sonnet regarding this matter.)

In Buddhism, they call this patient acknowledgment.

Life occurs regardless of your desires. This is the idea, all things considered. At the point when I acknowledged this, my disappointments liquefied away.

At the point when you can consider yourself to be an aspect of that nature, not isolated from it, and carry on as nature does, you will turn out to be more tranquil.

I've figured out how to grasp the work now.

The everyday. Nothing else matters, aside from my family. At the point when I'm with my child or my significant other, now I attempt to truly be available, to appreciate the now in every second.

At the point when I finish a post or a melody after numerous long periods of altering and cleaning it to a fine sparkle, I can remain back and grin. Another youngster is conceived. At that point I put it out into the world.

I wish for it to be a cheerful, thriving life as any mom would. I simply don't stress such a great amount of anything longer then I should or how everything turns out.

Everything always works out for me and ends up being great.

I was an Achievement Junkie? Here's How I started to enjoy the process

For as far back as I can recollect, I have defined a significant standard, found a way to accomplish said objective, and delighted in my prosperity and sentiments of self-authority. Tragically, my exclusive focus set on triumph has never permitted me to unwind into and appreciate the cycle, missing the devoted minutes between the accomplishments. Does this sound recognizable? Is it true that you are a self-declared accomplishment addict requiring an extensive recovery, ideally in a beachside office supplied with psychological wellness experts?

In the event that your response to that question is a resonating indeed, continue reading. The following are a few hints for easing back down and getting a charge out of the cycle while running after your objectives.

1. Stay rooted in the present, because it's a marathon, not a sprint.

At the point when I was running after another college degree, I was unable to stand by to proceed onward to another graduate school, a considerably more specific, genuine, intriguing and respectable program, I thought. The day after I moved on from my lord's program (truly, that program I wasn't possible with in light of the fact that I was so horrendously tired of school), I announced, "I think I need to get certifications now instead."

That was years prior, and in that time, I permitted myself to back off and move away from over-accomplishment and objective direction while I supported myself and investigated my interests.

While fixating on finish lines, I neglected to appreciate the races, races that looked considerably more like long distance races than the runs I portrayed them. (What's more,

I was a separation sprinter, so I should know better.)

Movement yourself. Slow down and be aware of the current second. That is typically where the enchantment occurs.

2. Practice self-awareness and take time to look within.

Thinking back, I frequently wish I could bounce into a time machine and return to my undergrad days as the me I am today, somebody who continually endeavors to value a mind-blowing snapshots, sinking into even extremely disrupting occasions. Some way or another, my objectives, regardless of their decency, turned into an approach to evade the second while accepting brief love pieces as awards from others (so I could adore myself). What's more, at last, my athletic undertakings turned into a route for me to metaphorically and in a real sense flee from what I didn't care for about myself.

The universe constrained me to sit still and go internal, and the main way it realized how to show this quick talking, speedy moving, over-achiever was to remove my legs from me as a neurological infection. I could no longer run from the reality of myself, and this drove me into a time of self-revelation that proceeds with today.

3. Enjoy the process.

This over-accomplishing character defect (on occasion, since objective direction can be very certain when utilized and not mishandled) even persisted to my encounters with this neurological sickness. My emphasis was on that supernatural occurrence fix, that unconstrained abatement that would happen in a moment on the off chance that I just did all that I "should do" to recuperate.

Mending was the ultimate objective that my sights were adamantly determined to and not once did I understand that the cycle was what truly made a difference, not the edgy objective of recuperating. Inevitably, the mending will come, however it will come in light of unwinding into and appreciating the cycle of thoughtfulness, self-revelation, self-realization and the acknowledging of my profound self.

4. Listen to your body.

How might you appreciate the progression on the off chance that you are in steady torment, be it physical or passionate? You simply should. You need to accumulate the quality, the tolerance and the interest to live at the time, regardless of whether the second is terrible.

Cry, kick and shout. Experience that terribleness, yet don't get some distance from it, or disregard it, or stuff it down to deteriorate inside your spirit as more disorder. It is that basic in principle, yet so troublesome practically speaking.

There are days when I actually battle, normally when every day obligations feel overpowering and time feels inadequate, however my manifestations never lie, and when they compound, I realize I am off course.

Your body is repeatedly talking to you. Tune in to its subtle messages. Self-awareness.

When you don't celebrate yourself or enjoy the process, that makes it difficult to celebrate others…then eventually a hater is born within you. Remember: They may want to be you but not everyone willing to work on themselves and do what it takes to be where you are in the core. Best investment ever is in yourself.

Conclusion

Becoming self-aware about the love you deserve changes your core from the inside to the out and gives you the freedom to externally express what was always inside you.

When did standards go out of style? Never forget how powerful you are. Date yourself, reward yourself, celebrate yourself. Most importantly, love yourself because you are worth it. Doing so may feel selfish to spend money and time on yourself because you've gotten used to doing for others first and yourself last, so a sense of guilt may come. You now have the tools and resources to process this, work through it, and get to the root of the issue. If you do this properly, your cup will be so full you can do for yourself and others at the same damn time. Trust me; it is always hard to pour from an empty cup. Don't believe me, try it literally. LOL. As human beings, we work the same way and have certain needs that are important for your cup to runneth over with love, joy, and empathy for others. An alternative would leave you stuck in the victim triangle. Water that self-love daily and stop conforming to what society tells us to do and listen to the one person you know you can trust. In other words, fuck external validation, what do you think of yourself? Nothing or no one will change that until you do. If you do not believe in yourself, you will be in situations where you can get 10 positive compliments and 1 negative. You will take in the negative one and doubt the 10 positive ones. After a while, that will eat you up inside and consume your mental and physical energy deeming yourself as unworthy. Guess what, when you have self-doubt, others doubt you as well. Eventually, you fight a losing battle against yourself with that same frame of mind. (Your subconscious is a computer that downloads everything you read, watch, the things said to you, experiences, as well as your environment. Your subconscious takes up 90% of your programming so you have to make a conscious decision with 10% to do things differently. 90% are habit-based and 10% is the part that changed the habits you become aware of and actively break.) OR (Subconscious- below awareness- 95% of time spent here - the software created in childhood (before full consciousness) that holds core beliefs, emotions, memories, behaviors and instincts. Your Conscious awareness is your highest self - authentic 'self' beyond conditioning, analytical mind, and habitual behavior love based, the soul, label-less, witness of the human experience.) Our daily habits become our life habits. Time for an upgrade on your computer programming in your brain. When dealing with your subconscious, remember positive and negative emotions cannot occupy the mind at the same time. One or the other most dominate. You have 7 positive emotions - desire, faith, love, sex, enthusiasm, romance, and hope. And 7 negative emotions - fear, jealousy, hatred, revenge, greed, superstition, and anger. Get faith over fear by feeling the fear and doing it anyway. Stop talking yourself out of new experiences, opportunities, and growth. We are all the same, we all need the same things, we all want some of the same things, and we all feel the same things...understand that and you now have empathy. Easier said than done, right? Be gentle with yourself and understand that you do not just wake up and become the butterfly, growth is a process. What is your why? That's a good place to start. What is your reason for getting up in the morning and pushing yourself to limits you never thought were possible? Mine is my son, he not only saved my life, but changed my worldview.

That will be important to remember when you want to give up at times. And know you do not have to be alone in this process. Start off by getting an accountability partner and surround yourself with like-minded people. You are the sum of the top 5 people you spend the most time around. Process these things, write the process out in your journal, then take the necessary steps toward a better version of yourself. Get to where you evolve so hard that you have to reintroduce yourself to people who thought they knew you. Believe in something bigger than yourself along the way, if you do not already.

I honestly had times where I didn't feel like a single thing was going right in my life, but you see, I have this vision...this beautiful vision. That vision always tells me that nothing in life is permanent, every single thing is temporary. From that papercut, you just got to the heartbreak that just happened. We have to remember this during those dark times late at night when we feel all hope is lost.

We have to believe; we have to find hope. Because that is where it all starts. Remember when we were younger, we could morph into any superhero character, be anything, conqueror the world all through our imaginations? Well, this is the most important time to live through your inner child. You see the things we enjoyed as children are still the things we enjoy now. We have just been "adulting" too much to think about it or enjoy those things. I loved to write, whether I was writing in my journal, making something creative, playing school, rap songs, scripts, making people laugh. Expressions! I fucking love to express myself in as many ways as possible because as simple as it may sound, it is not something I was allotted the opportunity to do growing up in the household of my family. So, I figured out ways to do those things anyway and I never knew how to specifically identify what I was trying to do. After going through this challenging life as an adult, I experienced the same feelings I felt as a child, which is just wanting to throw in the towel immediately...end it...die. So what is it I enjoyed doing as a child when I wanted to end it all then. The difference in then and now is I TRUST my faculties to lead me in the right direction. Now I want to add value, I want the world to be better because I was here.

I was asked this question, everything you experienced, worked on, accomplished, overcame...what did it lead to? They asked the question with their own answer in mind of believing that nothing came from it. I didn't take offense to it at all, I just realized I'm up against exactly what I thought I would be up against. My intent of this isn't to change who you are or lead you to believe that your way of doing things isn't right. Because what do we define as being wrong or right? Nothing is black and white; we tend to overlook the grey area in between and stopped acknowledging it. It is simplified down to just two choices. Even though we are genetically different with unique experiences and situations. So, no, this is not to force you to make my decision. This is just to give you another choice that could possibly be better. How can you live your best life out here in these streets if you never tried to maximize your full potential? How can you ever fully enjoy the being you were born to be at your best? Everyone can because we all have the freedom of choice to do so, and it is as simple as that. We may have different starting points in life, but we still all can make it to the finish line.

About the Author

"The more you know yourself, the more patience you have for what you see in others..."

– Erik Erikson

Malissa Penick is an entrepreneur and author who was born in Augsburg, Germany, the daughter of a US military serviceman. She grew up in Birmingham, Alabama, where she attended the University of Alabama in Birmingham where she attained a BA in Health Sciences and has a Master's in Business Administration.

Since then, Malissa has been on a journey through life, moving to San Diego then San Francisco Bay Area, getting more qualifications and starting her own business. She is currently in the process of moving back to her hometown of Birmingham, with her son, to be the change she wants to see in her community.

Aside from her business interests, Malissa has recently written her debut book, a self-help entitled ***Alive at 35***, which is aimed at helping people to overcome life traumas and negativity that has limited them in their quest for love and happiness.

In her free time, Malissa enjoys working out, dining out and vegging out with a good book and a generous glass of red wine. She also writes regularly, is passionate about lifelong learning and spends lots of time with her son. When she gets the chance she likes to travel and visit new and exciting places, meet new people and explore their cultures.

Malissa also does volunteer work, lending a hand where it is needed. She is constantly seeking to improve herself and can usually be found learning something new.

As far as the future goes, Malissa wants to improve the world and leave her own mark on it in whatever way she can. She intends to write more books that will concentrate on mental health, reaching out to as many people as possible, and to improve her business fortunes along the way.

You can contact or follow Malissa Penick at

Social Media: @malissapenick

Email: malissa@aliveatthirtyfive.com

Made in the USA
Monee, IL
04 November 2026

67384754R00095